Letts EDUCATIONAL

ADVANCED LEVEL

Revise A2 Computing

Author
Roger Legg

Contents

Specification lists

AQA Computing

MODULE	SPECIFICATION TOPIC	CHAPTER REFERENCE	STUDIED IN CLASS	REVISED	PRACTICE QUESTIONS
Module 4 (M4)	*Machine level structure, operation and assembly language programming*	*2.1–2.3*			
	Programming concepts	*6.1, 6.3–6.5, 7.1–7.7*			
	Data representation in computers	*3.1–3.3*			
	Operating systems	*4.1–4.4*			
Module 5 (M5)	*Applications and effects*	*1.1*			
	Databases	*5.3*			
	Systems development	*8.1–8.3*			
	Hardware devices	*1.2*			
	Networking	*9.1–9.4*			
Module 6 (M6)	*Systems development*	*8.1–8.3*			

Examination analysis

The specification comprises the three compulsory modules from the AS scheme of assessment and three compulsory modules (module 4, module 5 and module 6) from the A2 scheme of assessment.

Modules 4 and 5 will be assessed by written examinations that contain short answer questions and longer structured questions. All questions are compulsory. Module 6 will be assessed by a practical computing project.

Module 1 (AS)	*written paper*	*1 hr 30 min*	*17%*
Module 2 (AS)	*written paper*	*1 hr 30 min*	*17%*
Module 3 (AS)	*written paper*	*1 hr 30 min*	*17%*
Module 4	*written paper*	*1 hr 30 min*	*17%*
Module 5	*written paper*	*1 hr 30 min*	*17%*
Module 6	*coursework*		*15%*

Edexcel Computing

MODULE	SPECIFICATION TOPIC	CHAPTER REFERENCE	STUDIED IN CLASS	REVISED	PRACTICE QUESTIONS
Unit 4 (M4)	Relational database systems	5.3			
	File organisation	5.1, 5.2			
	Fourth-generation software tools	6.1			
	Computer hardware	1.2, 2.1–2.3			
	Communications	9.1–9.4			
	Systems software	4.1–4.4, 6.2, 6.:			
Unit 5 (M5)	Systems implementation strategies	8.1–8.3			
	Project management and the need for team working	8.4			
	Managing information	8.2			
	Data structures	3.2, 7.2–7.5			
	Algorithms	7.1, 7.6, 7.7			
	Programming	6.1, 6.3–6.5			
Unit 6 (M6)	Software design	8.2			
	Implementation	8.3			
	Testing	8.3			
	System documentation and evaluation	8.1			

Examination analysis

The specification comprises the three compulsory modules from the AS scheme of assessment and three compulsory modules (module 4, module 5 and module 6) from the A2 scheme of assessment.

Modules 4 and 5 will be assessed by written examinations that contain short answer questions and longer structured questions. All questions are compulsory. Module 6 will be assessed by a practical computing project.

Module 1 (AS)	written paper	1 hr 30 min	16.67%
Module 2 (AS)	written paper	1 hr 30 min	16.67%
Module 3 (AS)	coursework		16.67%
Module 4	written paper	1 hr 30 min	16.67%
Module 5	written paper	1 hr 30 min	16.67%
Module 6	coursework		16.67%

OCR Computing

MODULE	SPECIFICATION TOPIC	CHAPTER REFERENCE	STUDIED IN CLASS	REVISED	PRACTICE QUESTIONS
Module 4 (M4)	*The function of operating systems*	*4.1–4.4*			
	The function and purpose of translators	*6.2*			
	Computer architectures and the fetch-execute cycle	*2.1, 2.2*			
	Data representation, data structures and data manipulation	*3.2, 3.3, 7.1–7.7*			
	Programming paradigms	*6.1–6.5, 7.1*			
	Databases	*5.3*			
Module 5 (M5)	*Definition, investigation and analysis*	*8.1*			
	Design	*8.2*			
	Software development, testing and implementation	*8.3*			
	Documentation	*8.1*			
	Evaluation	*8.3*			
	Written report	*8.1–8.3*			
Module 6 (M6)	*Use of systems and data*	*1.1, 1.2*			
	Systems development, implementation, management and applications	*8.1–8.4*			
	Simulation and real-time processing	*1.1*			
	Common network environments, connectivity and security issues	*9.1–9.4*			

Examination analysis

The specification comprises the three compulsory modules from the AS scheme of assessment and three compulsory modules (module 4, module 5 and module 6) from the A2 scheme of assessment.

Modules 4 will be assessed by a written examination that contains 6–8 compulsory structured questions, some of which relate to a context. Module 6 will be assessed by a written examination that contains 5–7 compulsory structured questions set in the context of a short scenario. Module 5 will be assessed by a practical computing project.

Module 1 (AS)	*written paper*	*1 hr 30 min*	*15%*
Module 2 (AS)	*coursework*		*20%*
Module 3 (AS)	*written paper*	*1 hr 30 min*	*15%*
Module 4	*written paper*	*1 hr 30 min*	*15%*
Module 5	*coursework*		*20%*
Module 6	*written paper*	*1 hr 30 min*	*15%*

WJEC Computing

MODULE	SPECIFICATION TOPIC	CHAPTER REFERENCE	STUDIED IN CLASS	REVISED	PRACTICE QUESTIONS
Module 4 (CP4)	*System design*	*8.2, 8.3*			
	Representation of data as bit patterns	*3.1*			
	Logical operations	*2.3*			
	Algorithms	*7.1, 7.6, 7.7*			
	Data types and data structures	*3.2, 3.3, 7.2–7.5*			
	Software engineering	*6.1–6.5*			
Module 5 (CP5)	*The operating system*	*2.2, 4.1–4.4*			
	Input/output	*1.2*			
	Data transmission	*9.1*			
	Communication networks	*9.2–9.4*			
	Databases	*5.3*			
	Distributed systems	*9.2*			
	File organisation	*5.1, 5.2*			
	Typical applications of computers and communication systems	*1.1*			
	Data security and integrity processes	*8.2*			
	Disaster planning	*8.2*			
Module 6 (CP6)	*Feedback*	*8.1*			
	Design	*8.2*			
	Planning	*8.4*			
	Implementation	*8.3*			
	Maintenance documentation	*8.3*			
	Testing	*8.3*			
	Evaluation	*8.3*			
	User documentation	*8.3*			

Examination analysis

The specification comprises the three compulsory modules from the AS scheme of assessment and three compulsory modules (module 4, module 5 and module 6) from the A2 scheme of assessment.

Modules 4 and 5 will be assessed by written examinations that contain short answer questions and longer structured questions. All questions are compulsory. Module CP6 will be assessed by a practical computing project that develops the work done for module CP3.

Module CP1 (AS)	*written paper*	*2 hr*	*16.5%*
Module CP2 (AS)	*written paper*	*2 hr*	*16.5%*
Module CP3 (AS)	*coursework*		*17%*
Module CP4	*written paper*	*2 hr*	*16.5%*
Module CP5	*written paper*	*2 hr*	*16.5%*
Module CP6	*coursework*		*15%*

AS/A2 Level Computing courses

AS and A2

All Computing A Level courses being studied from September 2000 are in two parts, with three separate units or modules in each part. Most students will start by studying the AS (Advanced Subsidiary) course. Some will then go on to study the second part of the A Level course, called the A2. It is also possible to study the full A Level course, both AS and A2, in any order.

How will you be tested?

Assessment units

As well as being a choice of how the syllabuses are studied, there is also a choice of assessment. Of the three units that make up AS Computing, one contains some form of practical assessment. This may be a practical test set by the awarding body or it may be an assessment carried out by your teacher, based on the skills that you show on one or a number of practical tasks. Depending on the specification that you follow, part of a unit test may also be on an optional topic.

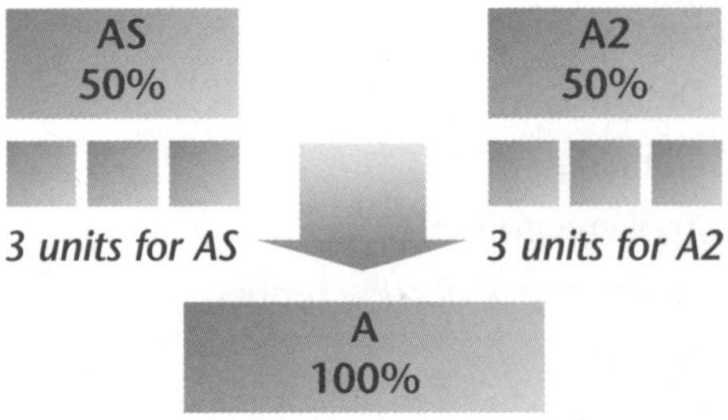

For AS Computing, you be tested by three assessment units. For the full A Level in Computing you will take a further three units. AS Computing forms 50% of the assessment weighting for the full A Level.

Each of these three tests can normally be taken in either January or June, so that you can take one or two tests part way through the course and leave the rest till the end or be assessed on the whole course when you have finished studying it. Any unit may be re-sat once.

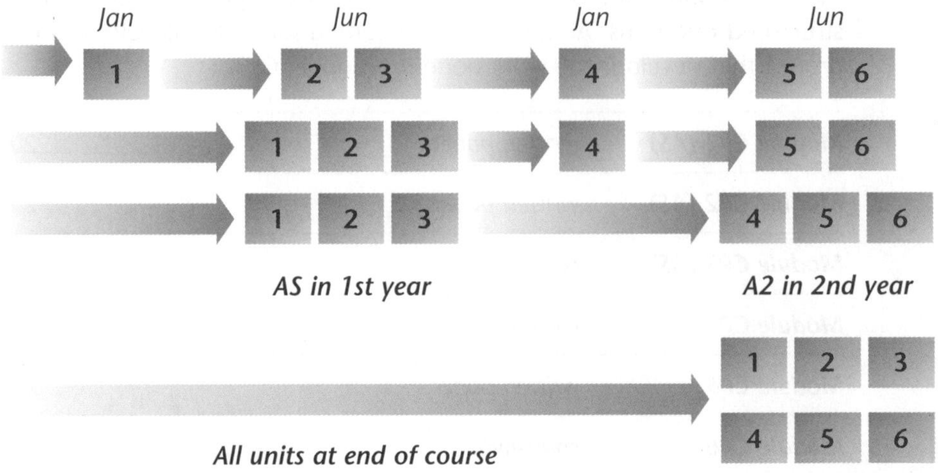

If you are disappointed with a module result, you can resit each module once. You will need to be very careful about when you take up a resit opportunity because you will have only one chance to improve your mark. The higher mark counts.

A2 and Synoptic assessment

For those students who, having studied AS, decide to go on to study A2, there are three further units to be studied. Similar assessment arrangements apply except some units, those that draw together various elements of the course in a 'synoptic' assessment, have to be assessed at the end of the course.

Coursework

Coursework will form part of your A Level Computing course. This will be in the form of a computing project that will assess your ability to design, test and implement a solution to a practical problem.

Key skills

It is important that you develop your key skills throughout the AS and A2 courses that you take, as these are skills that you need whatever you do beyond AS and A Levels. To gain the key skills qualification, which is equivalent to an AS Level, you will need to demonstrate that you have attained Level 3 in Communication, Application of number and Information technology. Part of the assessment can be done as normal class activity and part is by formal test.

It is a worthwhile qualification, as it demonstrates your ability to put your ideas across to other people, collect data and use up-to-date technology in your work.

What skills will I need?

Questions in A Level Computing examinations are designed to test a number of assessment objectives: these are skills and abilities that you should have acquired by studying the course. For the written papers at AS Level the main objectives being assessed are:

- recall of facts, terminology and relationships
- understanding of principles of operation of computer systems
- understanding of the application of computer systems
- explanation and interpretation of principles and concepts
- interpreting information given as numerical data or prose
- application of knowledge and understanding to familiar and unfamiliar situations.

Different types of questions in A2 examinations

In AS Computing examinations, different types of questions are used to assess your abilities and skills.

These include short-answer questions, structured questions requiring both short answers and more extended answers, together with case studies to which you have to apply your knowledge. Multiple choice question papers are not used, although it is possible that some short-answer questions will use a multiple choice format, where you have to choose the correct response from a number of given alternatives.

Short-answer questions

A short-answer question may test recall or it may test understanding by requiring you to undertake a short calculation. Short-answer questions often have space for the answers printed on the question paper. Here is an example (the answer is shown in purple):

In the context of data stored on a magnetic tape, what is meant by **each** of the following:

(i) field
(ii) record
(iii) file?

(i) A numeric value or string of characters representing a single item of data
(ii) All the fields relating to one person or a single object (e.g. a stock item)
(iii) An organised collection of related records

Structured questions

Structured questions are in several parts. The parts are usually about a common context and they often become progressively more difficult and more demanding as you work your way through the question. They may start with simple recall, then test understanding of a familiar or an unfamiliar situation. The most difficult part of a structured question is usually at the end, where the candidate is sometimes asked to suggest a reason for a particular phenomenon or social implication.

When answering structured questions, do not feel that you have to complete one question before starting the next. The further you are into a question, the more difficult the marks are to obtain. If you run out of ideas, go on to the next question. Five minutes spent on the beginning of that question are likely to be much more fruitful than the same time spent racking your brains trying to think of an explanation for an unfamiliar situation.

Here is an example of a structured question that becomes progressively more demanding.

(a) Draw a diagram showing how the microprocessor, data bus, address bus, control bus, memory and clock are interconnected in a computer system.

(b) Explain what hardware feature limits the amount of memory possible in a computer system.

(c) Describe **three** hardware design changes that would increase the speed of execution of programs.

Extended answers

In AS Level Computing, questions requiring more extended answers will usually form part of structured questions. They will normally appear at the end of structured questions and be characterised by having at least three marks (and often more) allocated to the answers as well as several lines (up to ten) of answer space. These questions are also used to assess your abilities to communicate ideas and put together a logical argument.

The 'correct' answers to extended questions are less well-defined than to those requiring short answers. Examiners may have a list of points for which credit is awarded up to the maximum for the question, or they may first of all judge the 'quality' of your response as poor, satisfactory or good before allocating it a mark within a range that corresponds to that 'quality'.

As an example of a question that requires an extended answer, a structured question on the use of storage devices could end with the following:

> Suggest why companies have chosen the CDROM as a suitable medium to distribute software and reference material. [8 marks]

Points that the examiners might look for include:

> The CD is read only so it is not going to be corrupted by users overwriting the information.
>
> The CD is extremely portable being light and fairly robust.
>
> It is not corrupted by magnetic fields so it does not have to be protected from them.
>
> It has a reasonable storage capacity, typically 640 Mbytes.
>
> The transfer speed is relatively slow but it is adequate for most purposes as the storage capacity is limited.

Full marks would be awarded for an argument that put forward four of these points in a clear and logical way.

Free-response questions

Little use is made of free-response and open-ended questions in A Level Computing. These types of question allow you to choose the context and to develop your own ideas. An example might be, 'Describe how you would introduce a new computer system incorporating point of sales terminals into a supermarket, taking care to minimise the disruption of day-to-day trading'. When answering this type of question it is important to plan your response and present your answer in a logical order.

Exam technique

Links from GCSE

Advanced Subsidiary Computing builds from grade C in GCSE Information technology. This study guide has been written so that you will be able to tackle A2 Computing from a GCSE Information technology background.

You should not need to search for important material from GCSE Information technology because this has been included where needed in each chapter. If you have not studied Computing for some time, you should still be able to learn A2 Computing using this text alone.

What are examiners looking for?

Examiners use instructions to help you to decide the length and depth of your answer. If a question does not seem to make sense, you may have misread it – read it again!

State, define, give or list

This requires a short, concise answer, often recall of material that can be learnt by rote.

Explain, describe or discuss

Some reasoning or some reference to theory is required, depending on the context.

Outline

This implies a short response, almost a list of sentences or bullet points.

Predict or deduce

You are not expected to answer by recall but by making a connection between pieces of information.

Suggest

You are expected to apply your general knowledge to a 'novel' situation, one which you have not directly studied during the AS Computing course.

Calculate

This is used when a numerical answer is required. You should always use units in quantities and significant figures should be used with care.

Look to see how many significant figures have been used for quantities in the question and give your answer to this degree of accuracy.

If the question uses 3 significant figures, then give your answer to 3 significant figures also.

Some dos and don'ts

Dos

Do answer the question.

- No credit can be given for a good answer that is irrelevant to the question.

Do use the mark allocation to guide how much you write.

- Two marks are awarded for two valid points – writing more will rarely gain more credit and could mean wasted time or even contradicting earlier valid points.

Do use diagrams, equations and tables in your responses.

- Even in 'essay-type' questions, these offer an excellent way of communicating Computing.

Do write legibly.

- An examiner cannot give marks if the answer cannot be read.

Do write using correct spelling and grammar. Structure longer essays carefully.

- Marks are now awarded for the quality of your language in exams.

Don'ts

Don't fill up any blank space on a paper.

- In structured questions, the number of dotted lines should guide the length of your answer.
- If you write too much, you waste time and may not finish the exam paper. You also risk contradicting yourself.

Don't write out the question again.

- This wastes time. The marks are for the answer!

Don't contradict yourself.

- The examiner cannot be expected to choose which answer is intended.

Don't spend too much time on a part that you find difficult.

- You may not have enough time to complete the exam. You can always return to a difficult calculation if you have time at the end of the exam.

What grade do you want?

Everyone would like to improve their grades but you will only manage this with a lot of hard work and determination. You should have a fair idea of your natural ability and likely grade in Computing and the hints below offer advice on improving that grade.

For a Grade A

You will need to be a very good all-rounder.

You must go into every exam knowing the work extremely well.

You must be able to apply your knowledge to new, unfamiliar situations.

You need to have practised many, many exam questions so that you are ready for the type of question that will appear.

The exams test all areas of the syllabus and any weaknesses in your knowledge will be found out. There must be no holes in your knowledge and understanding. For a Grade A, you must be competent in all areas.

For a Grade C

You must have a reasonable grasp of Computing but you may have weaknesses in several areas and you will be unsure of some of the reasons for the answers.

Many Grade C candidates are just as good at answering questions as the Grade A students but holes and weaknesses often show up in just some topics.

To improve, you will need to master your weaknesses and you must prepare thoroughly for the exam. You must become a better all-rounder.

For a Grade E

You cannot afford to miss the easy marks. Even if you find Computing difficult to understand and would be happy with a Grade E, there are plenty of questions in which you can gain marks.

You must memorise all definitions.

You must practise exam questions to give yourself confidence that you do know how to answer them. In exams, answer the parts of questions that you know first. You must not waste time on the difficult parts. You can always go back to these later.

The areas of Computing that you find most difficult are going to be hard to score on in exams. Even in the difficult questions, there are still marks to be gained. Show your working in calculations because credit is given for a sound method. You can always gain some marks if you get part of the way towards the solution.

What marks do you need?

The table below shows how your average mark is transferred into a grade.

average	*80%*	*70%*	*60%*	*50%*	*40%*
grade	*A*	*B*	*C*	*D*	*E*

Four steps to successful revision

Step 1: Understand

- Study the topic to be learned slowly. Make sure you understand the logic or important concepts.
- Mark up the text if necessary – underline, highlight and make notes.
- Re-read each paragraph slowly.

GO TO STEP 2

Step 2: Summarise

- Now make your own revision note summary:
  What is the main idea, theme or concept to be learned?
  What are the main points? How does the logic develop?
  Ask questions: Why? How? What next?
- Use bullet points, mind maps, patterned notes.
- Link ideas with mnemonics, mind maps, crazy stories.
- Note the title and date of the revision notes
  (e.g. Computing: File processing, 3rd March).
- Organise your notes carefully and keep them in a file.

This is now in short term memory. You will forget 80% of it if you do not go to Step 3.
GO TO STEP 3, but first take a 10 minute break.

Step 3: Memorise

- Take 25 minute learning 'bites' with 5 minute breaks.
- After each 5 minute break test yourself:
  Cover the original revision note summary.
  Write down the main points.
  Speak out loud (record on tape).
  Tell someone else.
  Repeat many times.

The material is well on its way to long term memory.
You will forget 40% if you do not do step 4. GO TO STEP 4

Step 4: Track/Review

- Create a Revision Diary (one A4 page per day).
- Make a revision plan for the topic, e.g. 1 day later, 1 week later, 1 month later.
- Record your revision in your Revision Diary, e.g.
  Computing: File processing, 3rd March 25 minutes
  Computing: File processing, 5th March 15 minutes
  Computing: File processing, 3rd April 15 minutes
  ... and then at monthly intervals.

Chapter 1
Applications

The following topics are covered in this chapter:

- *Typical applications*
- *Input/output*

1.1 Typical applications

After studying this section you should be able to:

LEARNING SUMMARY

- *discuss the application of computing in a variety of contexts*
- *discuss the extent to which a system satisfies the user's needs*
- *discuss the economic, legal and ethical consequences of the application*
- *describe a wide range of computing applications*
- *suggest package solutions when appropriate*

What you will need to know

AQA	M5
OCR	M6
WJEC	CP5

At A2 Level you should be aware of a range of applications and the effects these have on organisations, users and society. You will only obtain this knowledge by taking an interest in the way computers are used in society. You should observe how computers are used in shops, offices, and so on, and take note whenever they are mentioned in the media. You also need to ensure that you are familiar with the workings of a standard set of generic packages, i.e. a word-processor, a spreadsheet and a database.

The main difference between AS and A2 in this area is that the examiner will be expecting more detail in your answers.

You should be able to discuss the benefits of each application with which you are familiar. You should also appreciate the possible consequences of implementing such an application. A revision guide cannot cover all the applications that might occur. This guide attempts to point you to the areas that should be investigated. Many of the areas are covered in the AS Guide but there are some additional areas for A2.

You can only obtain a full understanding of this area by studying a wide range of current applications. You should be prepared for questions from any application area.

Safety-critical systems

This is a highly specialised field that involves the use of computers in safety-critical areas. These systems require a high level of dependability and so the development of safety-critical systems is a highly specialised field. Examples of safety-critical systems are:

- nuclear power station control systems
- railway signalling
- air traffic control
- 'fly by wire' aeroplane control systems.

Any application where there is a risk to people can be regarded as a safety-critical application.

These systems have to be specially tested to remove program bugs and they often have additional features built in to ensure safety. The main features are:

- programs have to be tested to higher standards
- duplication of essential systems are provided
- system must be 'fail-safe'.

Fail-safe means that, in the event of a system failure, the system will always return to a safe state; for example, a nuclear power station will shut down in the event of the failure of any part of the system.

Key points from AS

- **Types of application**
  Revise AS page 17
- **Application Software**
  Revise AS page 21
- **Implications**
  Revise AS page 23

> **KEY POINT**
> Safety-critical systems must be completely safe as lives may depend on them.

Control systems

This system will not recognise whether the sheet of metal is there or not.

Simple control systems respond to input sensors and produce an appropriate mechanical effect (Figure 1). For example, a robot to make car body parts may insert a sheet of metal and then press it to shape. If the metal sheet is too small or too large, the robot would not know.

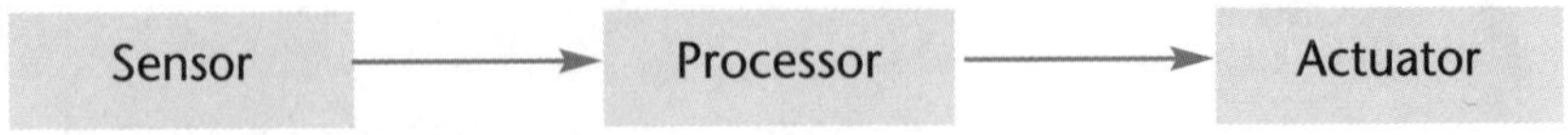

Figure 1 Simple control system

More sophisticated control systems use a method known as **feedback**. There will be sensors measuring the effect of each action and feeding this information back into the processor (Figure 2).

This system could recognise whether it has received a sheet of metal.

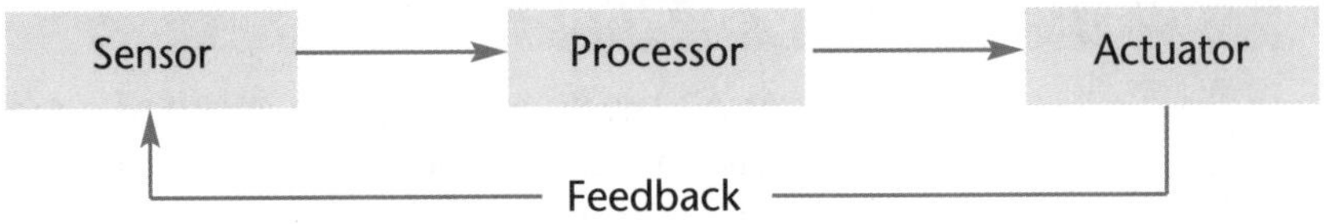

Figure 2

This allows the control system to react to the environment more effectively. An example might be a washing machine that fills with water until a certain level is reached.

> **KEY POINT**
> Control systems often use feedback to react in a more sophisticated way.

Progress check

An organisation intends to use a computerised light railway system to move parcels between different areas of its main site. The railway system will use driverless trains.

1 The computer system will use *feedback*. Explain what is meant by feedback in this context. [2]

2 Briefly describe **two** features which might be needed in a safety-critical computer system of this type. [2]

NEAB 1998

1 Previous actions of the system become input, which contributes to the selection of the next action. In this case there could be an automatic train control system that only allows a train onto a section of the track when there is no other train there.

2 The software must be rigorously tested to prove it is safe.
The critical parts of the system should be duplicated, e.g. the sensors on the track.
The system should be fail safe, i.e. the train's brakes should be applied in the case of a system failure.
[Any two of the above will get the marks.]

1.2 Input/output

After studying this section you should be able to:

LEARNING SUMMARY

- *explain how the application influences the input method*
- *discuss specific user-interface needs*
- *discuss the choice of output method*
- *explain how computers can be used when conventional input/output methods are inappropriate*
- *discuss methods for controlling machinery*

What you will need to know

AQA	M5
EDEXCEL	M4
OCR	M6
WJEC	CP5

It is difficult to prepare for these questions apart from being aware of all the possible devices that might be connected to a computer system.

Key points from AS

- **Input/output devices** *Revise AS page 36*
- **Operating systems** *Revise AS page 54*
- **Data entry** *Revise AS page 77*

This is an area where the examiner will be looking to discover whether you have a general knowledge of the various devices that can be used to interface between the computer system and the rest of the world. This will often be part of a larger question where you will be asked to apply your knowledge to a situation posed in the examination. A typical question will be to propose a situation where you will be asked to determine appropriate input and output devices or interfaces.

You are unlikely to obtain much credit for giving a list of possible devices – you will be expected to select the most appropriate. This skill can be achieved only by studying as wide a range of applications as possible.

KEY POINT

Study as many applications as possible and take particular note of the way the system interfaces with the rest of the world.

Progress check

1 A programming team has been asked to develop a suite of technical programs for use by scientists in a laboratory. It is intended that the suite of programs will control scientific equipment and will record results directly. The suite of programs will use a graphical user interface (GUI).

(a) Describe **three** benefits which a GUI would offer in this case over a text-based interface. [3]

(b) The suite of programs could instead have used an interface that used a mixture of GUI and text-based elements. Describe **four** possible benefits of being able to change from a GUI to a text-based interface on occasions. [4]

2 Most GUI systems use a *mouse*. State why a mouse is particularly suitable for a GUI system. [1]

1 (a) A graphical user interface will provide icons that will indicate to the user what programs are available.
The user will not have to remember the commands to operate the system, they can select from the menu options on the screen.
A new member of the team will need less training on a GUI than on a command line interface.
(b) It is essential to enter numerical data and/or descriptions of experiments.
The use of a GUI can often be slower than typing commands directly.
Several commands can be entered at once causing a sequence of actions to take place.
A password may need to be entered via a command line interface to ensure security of the system.
2 It allows the user to move a cursor over the screen to select the appropriate graphical component.

Sample questions and model answers

This is a typical question about an application. The production process implies robots and CAD/CAM. The examiner is trying to find out what you know about this area.

As there are three marks you only need to find three good points. If you can put down four you are unlikely to be penalised if one is wrong.

As there are only two marks, any two of the four points would get you full marks.

1

A manufacturing company is considering automating some of its production processes.

(a) Explain how computer systems can be used in the automation of production processes. [2]

(a) A CAD/CAM package will allow parts to be designed on the computer and the computer can then supply the commands to a robot to make them.

(b) (i) Give **three** benefits to the company of carrying out this automation. [3]

(b) (i) The quality of the finished product should be higher.
There will be reduced labour costs.
The health hazard of working with machinery is reduced.
The productivity will improve.

(ii) Give **two** implications for the company of carrying out this automation. [2]

(ii) There will be a training cost to operate the new equipment.
Money will have to be spent on the new equipment.
Maintenance costs will probably rise.
Redundancies may be necessary.

NEAB 2000, CP05

This type of question is quite common. You should be aware of the social and economic consequences of installing computer systems.

As above, a number of possible points are listed. You only need to provide three.

2

Replacing a manual system with a computerised system can have certain unwelcome consequences. Suggest three different examples of these unwelcome consequences at least **one** of which should be social and at least **one** economic. [3]

AEB 1997, Paper 1

Social consequences include:
loss of jobs; loss of skill; health consequences, e.g. repetitive strain injury (RSI); privacy of data; access to unacceptable material through the Internet, e.g. pornography.

Economic consequences:
cost of hardware and software; cost of staff training; maintenance cost to keep system up to date; cost of possible failure of system.

Any two sensible dangers that are not associated with the police or any other organisation that holds exempt data are required. Here are some examples.

There are a large number of possible answers. Any two of these points will get you the marks.

3

(a) Give **two** reasons why the storing of personal information that may not be exempt from the Data Protection Act 1984 could constitute a potential danger for the individual in society. [2]

(a) Credit card details might be used to commit fraud.
Hotel systems or telephone records might indicate where you have been.
This is an invasion of privacy.

(b) Police forces have access to vast amounts of information stored on computer systems. Briefly describe **two** ways in which the use of this information can help the police to combat crime. [2]

NEAB 1999, CP05

(b) Matching the details of a crime to the behaviour of known criminals
Can identify quickly the person wanted for questioning
Can identify the owner of a motor vehicle
Automatic fingerprint matching
Match evidence, e.g. paint found at scene can be analysed
Automatically keep track of police officers on patrol
A law database allows correct interpretation of the law.

Practice examination questions

1 Briefly describe **two** examples of how computers could aid surgeons performing operations. You must clearly show the role of the computer in your answer. [4]

AEB 1997, Paper 1

2 Briefly describe **four** ways in which computers could be used to manage the flow of administrative information within a school. [4]

NEAB 2000, CP05

3 Briefly describe an application where simulation by computer of a particular activity is important. In your answer you should include **two** reasons why this simulation is important to the organisation concerned and **two** benefits society gains from this simulation. [6]

NEAB 1998, CP05

4 In the following question, additional credit will be gained if your answer demonstrates skill in written communication.

A robotic vehicle is to be launched from Earth and sent to the moon to undertake exploration, including the analysis of minerals found on the moon's surface.

Describe how such a vehicle would be able to provide useful data for scientists on Earth and describe its benefits and drawbacks compared with sending human astronauts to the moon. [10]

WJEC specimen

Chapter 2

Computer architecture

The following topics are covered in this chapter:

- Computer processor
- Execution of machine code
- Assembly language

2.1 Computer processor

After studying this section you should be able to:

- *explain the role and operation of a processor*
- *describe the role of the components of a processor*
- *explain the effect of clock speed, word length and bus width on performance*

LEARNING SUMMARY

Processor components

AQA	M4
EDEXCEL	M4
OCR	M4

The configuration affects the instructions the processor can execute.

The main components of a processor are the arithmetic logic unit (ALU), the control unit and the registers. These are interconnected by a bus system.

There are many different types of processor. Some have a large number of registers and some have only a few. They also have more or less sophisticated bus structures. A typical configuration is illustrated in Figure 3.

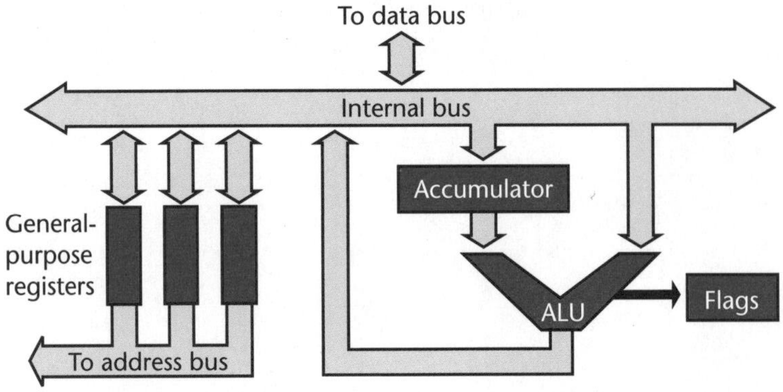

Figure 3

Arithmetic logic unit (ALU)

The ALU performs arithmetic and logic operations such as +, –, AND, OR, and so on. One of the inputs is from the accumulator and the other is from the internal bus in this configuration. The output can be directed to any of the registers. Some processors only allow the result of an arithmetic operation to be sent to the accumulator. In this case the configuration would be as shown in Figure 4.

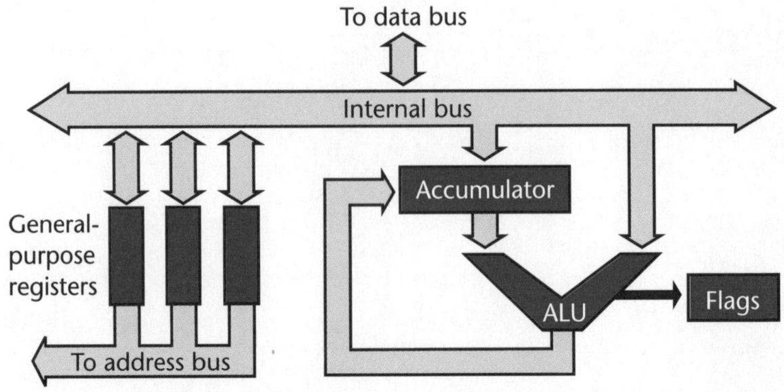

Figure 4

Key points from AS

- **Internal components of a computer system**
  Revise AS page 29

> Although there are many different types of processor they all have similar characteristics. They will all have an ALU, a number of registers and an internal bus.
>
> KEY POINT

Registers

The range and size of registers vary with different processors.

A register is a high-speed memory location within the processor. Most registers are general purpose but there are often some special registers with which you should be familiar.

- Accumulator is used for arithmetic and logic operations.
- Flags register is used to record the effect of the last ALU operation.
- Instruction register is used to hold the instruction that is currently being executed.
- Program counter holds the memory address of the current instruction.

Performance

AQA	M4
EDEXCEL	M4
OCR	M4

Performance can be affected by many factors. The major considerations are clock speed, word length and bus size.

Clock speed

A faster clock increases the speed of the processor and/or the memory, but not the peripherals.

The clock determines the timing for all operations. If the clock runs at a higher speed each operation will take less time and so the performance will be enhanced.

Word length

Increasing the word length of the registers has the greatest benefit to programs with many numerical calculations.

The word length is determined by the size of the registers and, generally speaking, a larger word size will give enhanced performance. Suppose we wish to perform an addition on two 64-bit numbers. If the registers are all 32 bits, each value will have to be stored in two registers and the calculation will involve two separate additions. If the registers were all 64 bits the amount of processing would be halved.

Bus width

Larger data buses improve data flow between the memory and the processor.

A wider bus will allow more bits to be transferred at one time. There have been computer systems produced where the registers were larger than the bus width. This gave high-speed calculations (as described above) but the transfer of data was slow owing to the number of transfers that had to take place.

> Performance is not solely determined by the clock speed. The word size and bus width must also be taken into account.
>
> KEY POINT

Progress check

1 Describe two design changes that can be made to a processor to improve its performance.

2 A microprocessor data bus has 16 lines and its address bus has 24 lines. What is the maximum memory capacity that can be connected to the microprocessor? [2]

AEB 1997, Paper 2

1 The clock speed can be increased to reduce the time taken to perform each operation.
The size of the data bus can be increased. This will allow more bits to be transferred each time memory is accessed. This will reduce the number of transfers required.

2 The address bus allows 2^{24} = 16 million locations.
The data bus allows each location to contain 16 bits. This allows up to 16 million 16-bit words to be connected.

2.2 Execution of machine code

After studying this section you should be able to:

- *describe the von Neumann machine*
- *describe the fetch/execute cycle in detail*
- *describe the use of interrupts*
- *explain the vectored interrupt system*
- *describe methods of performing parallel processing*

LEARNING SUMMARY

The von Neumann machine

AQA M4
EDEXCEL M4
OCR M4

This implies that a program must be in memory before it can be executed.

All modern computers are based on the ideas proposed separately by John von Neumann and Alan Turing in 1945. They suggested the stored-program concept. The proposal was that the program instructions that are to be executed and the data that are to be processed should both be stored in memory together. Computers based on this design are known as von Neumann machines. A von Neumann machine performs what is known as the fetch/execute cycle.

The fetch/execute cycle

AQA M4
EDEXCEL M4
OCR M4

When the computer is turned on it starts performing what is known as the fetch/execute cycle. The main memory will have coded program instructions and the purpose of the fetch/execute cycle is to execute these instructions. This process is described in outline form in the AS Guide, but for A2 you are required to understand the process in more detail. There are two registers – the memory address register (MAR) and the memory buffer register (MBR) – that are used to temporarily hold the data that are transferred through the address bus and the data bus, respectively (Figure 5).

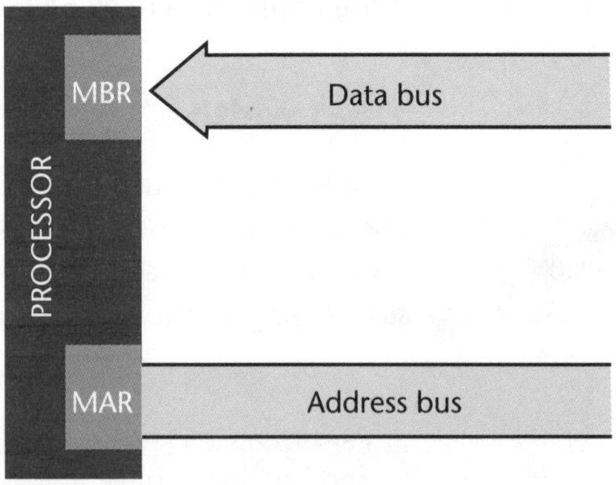

Figure 5

The fetch/execute cycle consists of the following steps:

1 Fetch
2 Decode
3 Execute.

The fetch/execute cycle is being performed all the time that the computer is switched on.

Fetch

1 The processor copies the contents of the program counter into the MAR.
2 The instruction is transferred via the data bus to the MBR.
3 The contents of the MBR are copied into the instruction register.

Key points from AS

- **Processor** *Revise AS page 30*
- **Machine code** *Revise AS page 103*

Decode

1 The instruction in the instruction register is decoded.

Execute

1 The program counter is updated to address the next instruction.
2 The instruction is executed.

In this manner the processor works its way through any program that is stored in the main memory.

> The processor's sole function is to perform the fetch/execute cycle.
>
> KEY POINT

Interrupt mechanism

AQA M4
EDEXCEL M4
WJEC CP5

The alternative is for the processor to continuously poll the devices.

Most modern computers provide a mechanism to allow devices (or programs) to interrupt the normal operation of the fetch/execute cycle as described above. An interrupt might be generated for a number of reasons but typical examples are:

- a mouse button has been pressed
- a disc transfer has just completed
- a timer needs to be updated
- a program has performed an illegal operation
- a piece of hardware has failed.

In each case an interrupt signal is generated and sent along a control wire to the processor.

Interrupt handling

The mechanism has to stop the current process at the end of an instruction, deal with the interrupt and then carry on as though nothing had happened.

Consider the situation when a mouse button is pressed. There will be a small program (called an interrupt handler or an interrupt service routine (ISR)) that will discover where the mouse is pointed and act accordingly. The user requires that this should happen immediately so the mechanism is to interrupt the program that is currently executing, perform the interrupt service routine and then return to the program. The process is as follows:

1 The instruction that is currently being executed must be allowed to finish its execution.
2 Interrupts are disabled. This prevents the interrupt service routine from being interrupted during execution (see priority of interrupts below).
3 The contents of the program counter (that contains the address of the next instruction to be executed in the interrupted program) are stored in memory.
4 The contents of all the other registers are stored in memory.
5 All interrupts are numbered and this allows the source of the interrupt to be identified.
6 The program counter is loaded with the address of the start of the appropriate interrupt service routine.
7 The interrupt service routine is executed.
8 The contents of the registers that were saved in step 4 are retrieved from memory.
9 The program counter is restored from memory so that it addresses the next instruction in the interrupted program.
10 Interrupts are restored.

You can get a device conflict when two devices try to use the same interrupt vector.

Vectored interrupts

Interrupts are numbered and this number is known as the interrupt vector. The interrupt vector is used to select the appropriate interrupt service routine. The addresses of the interrupt service routines are stored in an array (known as the interrupt despatch table) and the interrupt vector is used as a subscript to this array (Figure 6).

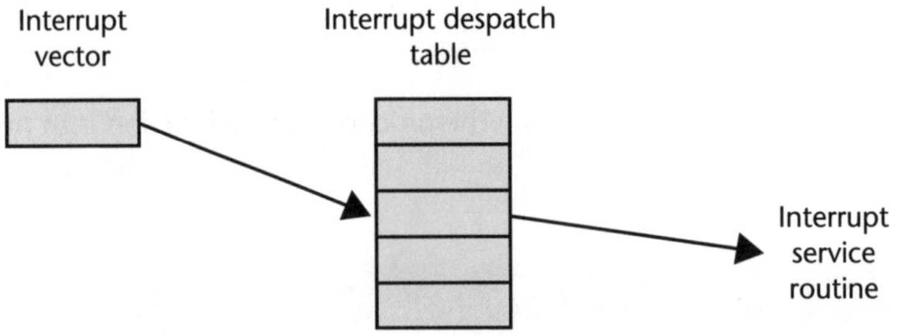

Figure 6

Priority of interrupts

Some interrupts are more urgent than others, so it is common practice to give interrupts a priority level. In this case the processor will allow a higher-priority interrupt to interrupt a lower-priority interrupt but not vice versa. To allow this to happen, steps 2 and 10 become:

2 Interrupts of a lower priority are disabled.
10 Interrupts of a lower priority are restored.

> **KEY POINT**
> An interrupt service routine is a subroutine that is called when an interrupt occurs.

Parallel processing

AQA M4
EDEXCEL M4

A problem with the von Neumann machine is that there is a limit to the speed at which it can process instructions. Electronic components can only operate at the speed of light and computers are now so fast that this limit is being reached. The von Neumann machine executes instructions serially, i.e. one after the other, and is known as a single instruction stream single data stream (SISD) computer. An SISD computer will be limited by the time it takes to process each instruction. What is needed is some method of executing instructions in parallel, i.e. doing more than one thing at the same time.

Pipelining

Pipelining is now common in most processors.

A pipelined processor overlaps the various stages of the fetch/execute cycle. While it is executing an instruction it can be fetching the next instruction at the same time. This is still an SISD computer but it can execute instructions much more quickly.

Vector (array) processing

Parallel processing is widely used in weather forecasting and enhancement of pictures received from space.

A processor can be made with several ALUs. This allows it to process all the elements in an array at the same time. This is known as a vector processor or an array processor. It is classified as a single instruction stream multiple data stream (SIMD) computer.

Multiple processors

A number of separate processors can be connected in such a way that they can perform instructions in parallel to solve a single problem. This is classified as a multiple instruction stream multiple data stream (MIMD) computer.

KEY POINT

By performing operations in parallel it is possible to improve the performance of a computer system.

Progress check

1 (a) What is meant by an interrupt? [2]

(b) Give two examples of the causes of interrupts [2]

(c) After installing a CD-ROM device to a personal computer, an error message 'interrupt conflict' appears. What is the likely cause of the problem? [2]

NEAB 2000, CP05

2 Name two registers that are involved in the fetch part of the fetch/execute cycle and describe how they are used.

1 (a) A signal from a device (or a process) that indicates that the device (or process) needs attention.
(b) A disk may generate an interrupt when a read or write is complete.
A keyboard may generate an interrupt when a key is pressed.
(c) The interrupt associated with the CD-ROM is already being used by another device or process.

2 The memory address register (MAR) is used to place the address of the instruction onto the address bus.
The memory buffer register (MBR) is used to store the data that are transferred from memory via the data bus.
[The program counter (or instruction pointer) is an alternative answer.]

2.3 Assembly language

After studying this section you should be able to:

LEARNING SUMMARY

- *explain the relationship between machine code and assembly code*
- *describe the nature and format of assembly code instructions*
- *illustrate their use for elementary machine operations*
- *describe the various modes of addressing memory*

Machine code

AQA M4
EDEXCEL M4

All computers execute machine code programs. A machine code instruction consists of a binary code that represents an operation optionally followed by one or more addresses (known as operands). An instruction to move data from 0000110000001111 to 0000110000001100 might be:

01101001	0000110000001111	0000110000001100
MOVE operation	Address 1	Address 2

Although this operation may be called MOVE, the data are in fact copied from one place to another.

Assembly language instructions

AQA M4
EDEXCEL M4
WJEC CP4

Assembly language instructions are translated to machine code by an assembler program.

It is very difficult for humans to work in machine code so assembly language has been developed. An assembly language instruction has a mnemonic (a shorthand description) to describe the operation and allows the programmer to name memory locations. The machine code instruction above might be written as:

```
MOV     INAMOUNT, OUTAMOUNT
```

Copy instructions

There will always be instructions that allow data to be copied from one place to another. Typical examples are MOV (short for MOVE), LD (short for LOAD), ST (short for STORE). An example of a MOV instruction is given above.

Arithmetic instructions

Multiplication can be performed by repeatedly adding.

A simple processor may only offer ADD and SUB (short for SUBTRACT). More sophisticated processors will have a MUL (MULTIPLY) and DIV (DIVIDE). Often, arithmetic can only be performed in the accumulator (often known as A). In this case the instructions to add up values stored in locations X and Y and store the result in location Z might be:

```
MOV   X,A   Copy the contents of X into the accumulator
ADD   Y     Add the contents of Y to the accumulator
MOV   A,Z   Store result in Z
```

Key points from AS

- **Buses**
  Revise AS page 29
- **Magnetic disk**
  Revise AS page 33
- **Assembly language**
  Revise AS page 103

Jump instructions

Each instruction can be given a label. There is an unconditional jump instruction that causes a labelled instruction to be executed next. An example might be:

```
JP      NEXT  Jump to the instruction labelled NEXT
```

There are also conditional jump instructions. Conditional jump instructions are

A jump is equivalent to a goto in a high-level language. Gotos are not necessary in high-level languages and should not be used but they are necessary in assembly code.

similar to IF instructions in a high-level language. A conditional jump is normally used in conjunction with a compare instruction. The compare instruction sets the flags register and the conditional jump tests the value of the flags. An example is:

CP	A,B	Compare A with B (this instruction sets the flags)
JE	L1	Jump if equal to the instruction labelled L1

Logical instructions

There are four logical instructions:

- NOT
- AND
- OR
- XOR

Logical instructions are used to manipulate bits.

They are known as bit-wise operations, i.e. they operate on all the individual bits in binary values. The effects are as follows.

The NOT instruction operates on a single binary value. The effect is to change each 1 to 0 and each 0 to 1. This can be described by a truth table:

Input	0	1
Result of NOT	1	0

An example of its use on an 8-bit value is:

NOT	10001110
gives	01110001

The AND, OR and XOR instructions each operate on a pair of binary values. In each case the operations are performed bit by bit.

The AND instruction produces a 1 if both the bits are 1. In every other case a 0 is produced. This can be described by a truth table:

	Input 1: 0	Input 1: 1
Input 2: 0	0	0
Input 2: 1	0	1

An example of its use on two 8-bit values is:

	11001011
AND	01100110
gives	01000010

The OR instruction produces a 1 if either of the bits is 1. This can be described by a truth table:

	Input 1: 0	Input 1: 1
Input 2: 0	0	1
Input 2: 1	1	1

An example of its use on two 8-bit values is:

	11001011
OR	01100110
gives	11101111

The XOR instruction produces a 1 if the two bits are different. If they are the same a 0 is produced. This can be described by a truth table:

	Input 1: 0	Input 1: 1
Input 2: 0	0	1
Input 2: 1	1	0

An example of its use on two 8-bit values is:

	11001011
XOR	01100110
gives	10101101

The AND instruction is used to turn bits off (i.e. change them to 0), the OR instruction is used to turn bits on (i.e. change them to 1) and the XOR is used to compare values.

Shift instructions

Shift instructions move all the bits in a value to the right or left. There are three main types of shift instruction:

Logical shifts are used to move a bit (or bits) to a specific place.

- logical shift
- arithmetic shift
- cyclical shift or rotation.

Logical shifts simply shift the value and place a 0 in the empty position. The bit that is shifted out of the value is lost. Examples are:

Shift right logical

1 1 0 1 1 1 0 1 becomes 0 1 1 0 1 1 1 0

Shift left logical

1 1 0 1 1 1 0 1 becomes 1 0 1 1 1 0 1 0

Shift right logical

0 0 0 1 1 1 0 1 becomes 0 0 0 0 1 1 1 0

Shift left logical

0 0 0 1 1 1 0 1 becomes 0 0 1 1 1 0 1 0

An arithmetic shift left multiplies the value by 2. An arithmetic shift right divides the value by 2.

Arithmetic shifts maintain the sign of the arithmetic value. Examples are:

Shift right arithmetic

1 1 0 1 1 1 0 1 becomes 1 1 1 0 1 1 1 0

Shift left arithmetic

1 1 0 1 1 1 0 1 becomes 1 0 1 1 1 0 1 0

Shift right arithmetic

0 0 0 1 1 1 0 1 becomes 0 0 0 0 1 1 1 0

Shift left arithmetic

0 0 0 1 1 1 0 1 becomes 0 0 1 1 1 0 1 0

Rotates are used to place bits in specific positions without losing any of the other bits.

Rotations, as their name suggests, rotate the bits and no bits are lost. Examples are:

Rotate right

1 1 0 1 1 1 0 1 becomes 1 1 1 0 1 1 1 0

Rotate left

1 1 0 1 1 1 0 1 becomes 1 0 1 1 1 0 1 1

Addressing modes

AQA M4
EDEXCEL M4

An operand in an assembly code instruction is in the form of an address, that is a number that represents some part of the computer system. This address can be formed in various different ways. Common methods are:

- immediate
- direct
- indirect
- indexed
- base register.

Immediate addressing

This might be used to address a constant value.

This is not really an address at all. The operand contains a value that is to be used in the instruction. An example might be:

ADD A, #5 Add 5 to the accumulator – 5 is an immediate address

Direct addressing

The operand contains the address of the memory location to be used (Figure 7).

This might be used to address a memory variable.

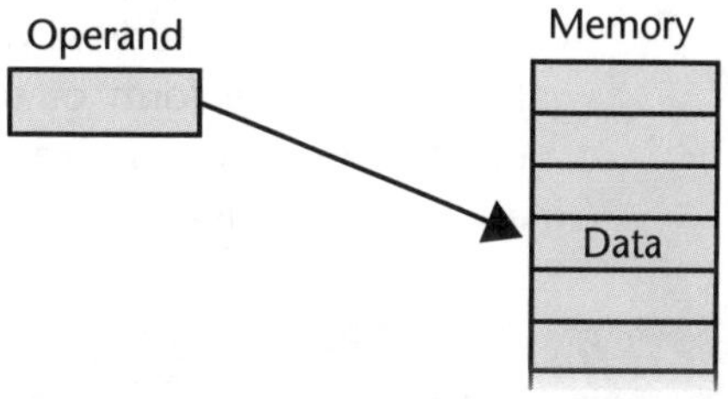

Figure 7

Indirect addressing

The operand contains the address of a memory location that contains the address of the memory location that contains the data to be used (Figure 8).

An array is stored as the address of the first element. Another use is a parameter that is passed by reference (a var parameter in Pascal).

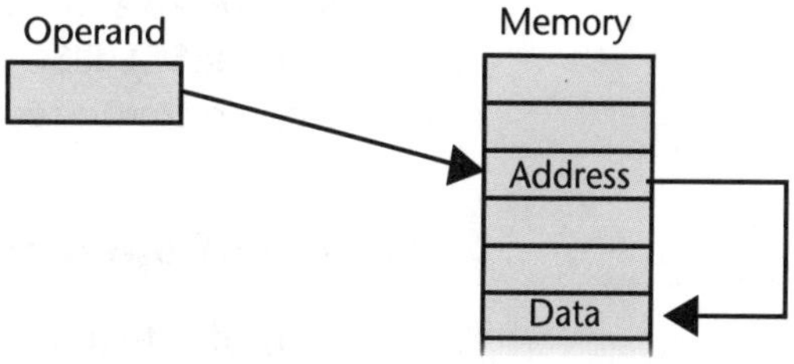

Figure 8

Index register addressing

An address is held in an index register. The operand contains an offset that is added to the value in the index register to obtain the required memory address. Alternatively, the index register can contain the offset and the operand can contain the address (Figure 9).

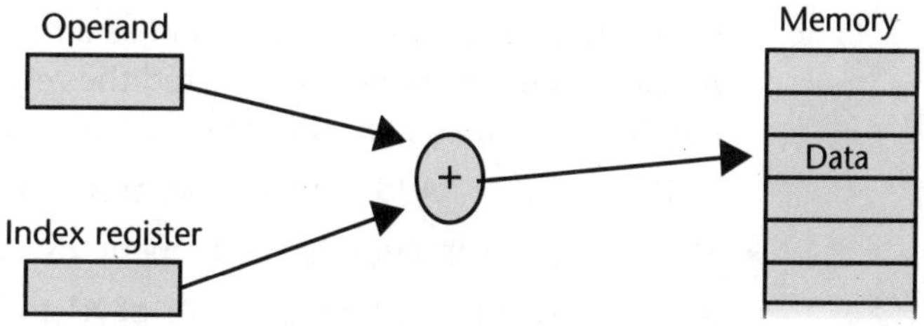

Figure 9

One use of indexed addressing is to process arrays. The operand is set to address the start of the array and the offset can be associated with the index register.

Another use of indexed addressing is to process a record that contains several fields. The index register can be set to address the start of the record and the operand can contain the offset of the required field from the start of the record.

Base register addressing

Base register addressing is similar to index register addressing. A base address is held in a base register. The operand contains an offset that is added to the value in the base register to obtain the required memory address (Figure 10).

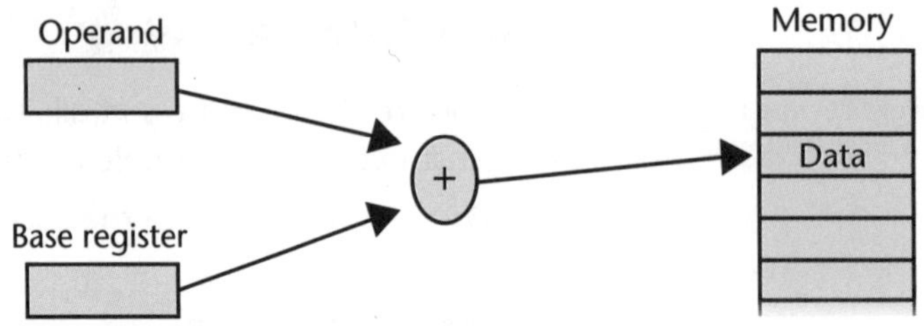

Figure 10

The difference between base addressing and index addressing is in the way they are used. A base address will normally apply to the whole program. Addresses can then be in the form of offsets from the start of the program. This allows the operating system to locate a program anywhere in memory by setting the base address accordingly.

Instruction categories

AQA M4
EDEXCEL M4

Over the years there have been many different families of processors, each with their own set of instructions. One way of making a processor more powerful is to make each instruction more complex. This results in what is known as a complex instruction set computer (CISC). It was discovered that most applications use only a small portion of the available instructions. By limiting the range of instructions it is possible to make a simpler and faster computer known as a reduced instruction set computer (RISC). RISC processors tend to have more registers thereby allowing more use of register-to-register operations.

Number of operands

Another way of categorising instruction sets is by the number of operands in each instruction.

- Zero address instruction has no operands. One address is usually implied, for example:

  CLA Clear accumulator

- One address instruction has one operand. Normally a second address is explicit. An example is:

  ADD X1 Add the contents of X1 to the accumulator

- One and a half address instruction has a register as one of the two operands. As the number of registers is limited the register can be identified with a small number of bits, known as a short address. An example is:

  ADD A,X Add the contents of X to the accumulator

- Two address instruction has two operands. An example is:

  ADD Y2,X1 Add the contents of X1 to Y2

- Three address instruction has three operands. An example is:

  ADD X2,Y2,X1 Add the contents of X1 to the contents of Y2 and store the result in X2

Progress check

This type of question requires you to carefully work through the code noting down the effect of each instruction.

1 (a) Use the following example of 8-bit binary representation to demonstrate a logical shift left. [1]

1	0	0	1	1	1	0	1

(b) Draw up a truth table to demonstrate the operation of an AND gate. [2]

(c) A simple computer has a number of 8-bit registers.
The instruction set includes the following:

LDA	R,N	Loads register R with value N
ADD	R,N	Adds value N to register R
SUB	R,N	Subtracts value N from register R
STO	R1,R2,A	Stores the contents of register R1 in address A, indexed by register R2
JNZ	R,L	Jump to label L if content of register R is not equal to 0
HLT		Halts execution

(i) Describe in words the effect of the following instructions:

```
LDA   2,5
ADD   2,4
```

[2]

(ii) Copy the trace table below, then trace the effect of the following code in the table. The effect of instruction [1] is already shown in the table.

```
[1]      LDA   1,0
[2]      LDA   2,4
[3]   L: ADD   1,2
[4]      SUB   2,1
[5]      STO   1,2,2000
[6]      JNZ   2,L
[7]      HLT
```

Register		Memory address			
R_1	R_2	2003	2002	2001	2000
0					

[5]

WJEC 1998, C3

answers overleaf

Progress check (continued)

1 (a)

0	0	1	1	1	0	1	0

(b)

		Input 1	
		0	1
Input 2	0	0	0
	1	0	1

(c) (i) LDA 2,5 will load the value 5 into register 2

ADD 2,4 will add 4 to the contents of register 2

If these two instructions are executed one after the other the result will be a value of 9 in register 2.

(ii)

Register		Memory address			
R1	R2	2003	2002	2001	2000
0					
	4				
2					
	3				
		2			
4					
	2				
			4		
6					
	1				
				6	
8					
	0				
					8

Sample questions and model answers

1

(a) Draw up truth tables to demonstrate the following:

(i) the AND operation [2]

(a) (i)

		Input 1	
		0	1
Input 2	0	0	0
	1	0	1

(ii) the NOT operation. [1]

(ii)

Input	
0	1
0	0

(b) (i) Carry out an AND operation of the following two 12-bit numbers:

A = 110101010111
M = 000000000010 [2]

(b) (i)

110101010111
<u>000000000010</u>
000000000010

(ii) Describe in words the effect of ANDing any 12-bit number with the number M. [1]

(ii) All the bits except bit 1 (the bit next to the least significant bit) will be set to 0. Bit 1 will remain as it was before the AND operation.

(c) It is now less common to use assembly language in computer programming than it was some years ago.

(i) Explain why this is the case. [1]

(c) (i) There are alternative languages that are easier to use. Assembly code can only be used on one range of processors so it is limited in its application.

(ii) Explain why assembly language is still used in some applications. Give **one** example of such an application. [2]

(ii) Assembly language is used when the fastest possible program is needed or when it is impossible to write the program in a high-level language. An example would be programming a computer game that requires high-speed graphics.

WJEC 2000, C3

Sample questions and model answers (continued)

2

A certain computer has the following instruction code format.

INSTRUCTION	ADDRESSING MODE	OPERAND

The following diagrams depict the contents of various memory locations and registers inside this computer.

Location 21_{10}	25_{10}	index register	7_{10}
Location 25_{10}	28_{10}		
Location 28_{10}	75_{10}		Accumulator

(a) State the contents of the accumulator after each of the following instructions.

(i)

Load Accumulator	Direct	21_{10}	[1]

(a) (i) 25_{10}

(ii)

Load Accumulator	Immediate	21_{10}	[1]

(ii) 21_{10}

(iii)

Load Accumulator	Indexed	21_{10}	[1]

(iii) 75_{10}

(iv)

Load Accumulator	Indirect	21_{10}	[1]

(iv) 28_{10}

(b) State a use of:

(i) indexed addressing [1]

(b) (i) Processing an array.

(ii) indirect addressing. [1]

(ii) Passing parameters by reference (var parameters in Pascal) or an array is normally stored as an indirect address to the first element.

EDEXCEL 2000, Paper 2

Practice examination questions

1 (a) Explain how each of the following can lead to faster execution of instructions in a computer:

(i) modifying the width of the data bus [1]

(ii) altering the clock rate. [1]

(b) State one other feature of processor design or configuration which improves processor performance and describe how the improvement is achieved. [2]

AEB 1998, Paper 3

2 (a) Draw up a truth table to demonstrate the **EXCLUSIVE OR (XOR)** operation. [2]

(b) (i) Carry out a bit-wise **XOR** operation on the following two 8-bit binary numbers: [2]

X = 10001011
K = 11100010

(ii) State what the results would be if you carried out a bit-wise **XOR** on your answer to part b(i) and the number **K**. [1]

WJEC CP4, Specimen

3 (a) What is an interrupt? [2]

(b) Give **two** reasons why an interrupt might occur. [2]

AEB 1997, Paper 2

4 Explain *base addressing* and its role in a multiprogramming operating system. [5]

AEB 1999, Paper 3

Chapter 3

Data representation

The following topics are covered in this chapter:

- Representation of data as bit patterns
- Data structures
- Implementation of data structures

3.1 Representation of data as bit patterns

After studying this section you should be able to:

- describe how an unsigned real number is represented in fixed-point form in binary
- describe the use of two's complement to perform subtraction
- discuss the trade-off between accuracy and range when representing numbers
- explain the effects upon accuracy of truncation and rounding
- describe the causes of overflow and underflow

LEARNING SUMMARY

Fixed point binary

AQA M4

The binary point is in a fixed position so it does not have to be stored in memory.

Key points from AS

- **Coding of data**
  Revise AS pages 41–49

Numbers are separated into integers (whole numbers) and real numbers (numbers with digits after the decimal point). A real number can be held in a fixed format with a fixed number of bits and a binary point in a fixed position. The value 10.75 is represented in binary as 1010.11, as follows:

8	4	2	1	.	½	¼
1	0	1	0	.	1	1

Let us consider a fixed point format of 16 bits with a binary point in the middle (i.e. after the eight most significant bits). This value can be stored using this format as follows:

0	0	0	0	1	0	1	0	1	1	0	0	0	0	0	0

A binary point is implied at this point

The problem with fixed point format is that the range and accuracy of values stored are limited. For this reason the floating point format is generally preferred as it maximises the range and values that can be stored in a fixed number of bits.

This method has generally been replaced by the floating point representation.

KEY POINT

Subtraction using two's complement

AQA M4

Two's complement as a method of storing values is described in the AS Guide. The main purpose of two's complement representation is that the addition of positive and negative numbers is made simple. If we take the values 7 and –5, these are represented in eight bits as follows:

It is relatively straightforward to provide an adding circuit.

7 becomes 00000111
–5 becomes 11111011

If we add these two values together we get

```
   0 0 0 0 0 1 1 1
 + 1 1 1 1 1 0 1 1
 1 0 0 0 0 0 0 1 0
```

This cannot be stored in the eight bits

As you can see this gives the correct result in the eight bits of the result.

> **KEY POINT**
> When processors perform subtraction they often convert the number to its negative form using two's complement format and then perform addition.

Truncation and rounding

WJEC CP4

Strictly speaking, truncating means removing the digits, and rounding is an option of when truncation takes place.

It is sometimes necessary to remove digits when values are made to fit into a fixed format. This may be because they are being transferred from a format that allows more digits to be stored or because of the effects of arithmetic operations. When this is necessary, the least significant digits (i.e. from the right-hand end) have to be removed. These can be removed by truncating the value or by rounding.

Truncation

Truncation is normally taken to mean that digits are simply removed. If a large number of truncations are involved in computing a result then the final value might be noticeably reduced.

Rounding

When rounding is performed, the least significant digit in the result may be increased by one depending on the digit(s) removed. The result should represent the value that is nearest to the original value. Examples are:

28.22 rounded to 3 significant digits becomes 28.2
28.25 rounded to 3 significant digits becomes 28.3
28.28 rounded to 3 significant digits becomes 28.3
5449 rounded to 2 significant digits becomes 5400
5450 rounded to 2 significant digits becomes 5500

The rule is that if the most significant digit being removed is 5 or above, 1 is added to the least significant digit in the result. This can also be applied to binary values. In this case 1 is added to the least significant bit in the result if the most significant bit removed is a 1. Examples are:

1100 rounded to 3 significant digits becomes 1100
1101 rounded to 3 significant digits becomes 1110
1110.1101 rounded to 6 significant digits becomes 1110.11
1110.1110 rounded to 6 significant digits becomes 1111.00

> **KEY POINT**
> Both methods remove the least significant digits, but when numbers are rounded the resulting digits may be adjusted.

Overflow and underflow

WJEC CP4

No matter how numbers are stored in the computer there is always a limit to the range of numbers that can be stored. If a result is computed that is outside the range of possible values we say that overflow or underflow has occurred.

Integers

Overflow occurs when a large number is divided by a small number or when two large numbers are multiplied together.

In the case of integers the range of numbers is continuous. If a result is outside the possible range we say that overflow has occurred.

Overflow	Valid result	Overflow
–		+

Floating point

Underflow occurs when a small number is divided by a large number or when two small numbers are multiplied together.

In the case of floating point (or fixed point binary) the situation is rather more complicated. In this case there is a largest and smallest positive value and also a largest and smallest negative value that can be stored. In between, around 0, there is a range of values that cannot be stored. If a computation produces a number that is in this gap we say that underflow has occurred. A result that is totally outside the range of values still produces overflow.

Overflow	Valid result	Underflow	Valid result	Overflow
–		0		+

KEY POINT

Overflow and underflow occur when the result of a calculation falls outside of the range of values permitted by the representation of the number.

Progress check

1 (a) Explain the terms overflow and underflow when applied to floating point representation.
(b) Give an example of a calculation that might cause
(i) overflow
(ii) underflow.

2 For **each** of the following binary values, give the result of
(a) rounding to two significant figures
(b) truncating to two significant figures
(i) 100.1
(ii) 10101
(iii) 11011
(iv) 11.101

1 (a) Overflow occurs when a computation produces a large positive result that is outside the range of values that can be stored. It also occurs when a result is produced that is so large and negative that it cannot be stored.
Underflow occurs when a result is too close to 0 to be stored.
(b) (i) Overflow occurs when a large value is divided by a very small value.
(ii) Underflow occurs when a very small value is divided by a very large value
2 (a) (i) 100
(ii) 11000
(iii) 11000
(iv) 100
(b) (i) 100
(ii) 10000
(iii) 11000
(iv) 11

3.2 Data structures

After studying this section you should be able to:

LEARNING SUMMARY

- *explain what is meant by a data structure*
- *describe the common data structures: sets, lists, stacks, queues, trees*
- *select appropriate data structures for given situations*

A data structure consists of a number of values and a number of operations. It is said that a data structure is defined by its operations, and this is how it differs from normal variables that are used in a program. We are not concerned as to the method used to store the data so long as the operations are successful. The algorithms for the data structure operations that you might need to know are to be found in Chapter 7.

We could consider a file on a disk to be a data structure. There are a limited number of operations that can be performed on a file: typically open, close, read and write. As a user of a file you are not concerned about how the data are organised so long as the operations function correctly.

Set

EDEXCEL M5

Some programming languages have a set data structure included as part of the language.

A set is a collection of items in no particular sequence. Typical operations on a set are:

- Add – to add an item to the set
- Remove – to remove an item from a set
- Isin – to determine whether an item is in the set.

A set might be used in a situation where a number of items need to be collected together. The program can then easily check to discover whether an item is a member of the set using the Isin operation.

List

AQA M4
EDEXCEL M5
OCR M4
WJEC CP4

The list is known as a linear data structure as you can imagine the list being a line of data items.

A list is a collection of items that are normally stored in the order that they are added. It can store items in a particular sequence if required but this will depend on the operations that are defined. A typical list might have the following operations:

- Insert – insert an item into the list
- First – obtain first item in the list
- Next – obtain the next item in the list
- Delete – remove an item from the list
- Locate – obtain the position of an item in the list.

The list is a basic data structure that can be used to implement other linear structures, such as Stack and Queue.

Stack

AQA M4
EDEXCEL M5
OCR M4
WJEC CP4

All modern computers have a system stack, and Push and Pop are standard machine code instructions.

A stack is a last in first out (LIFO) data structure. It normally has the following operations:

- Push – add an item to the top of the stack
- Pop – remove an item from the top of the stack
- Top – obtain the item at the top of the stack.

Stacks are widely used whenever it is required to retrieve the items in the reverse order to the order they were added.

Queue

AQA M4
EDEXCEL M5
OCR M4
WJEC CP4

As well as being widely used by the operating system, a queue might be used by a simulation program, for example a queue at traffic lights.

A queue is a first in first out (FIFO) data structure. It will normally have the following operations:

- Add – add an item to the back of the queue
- Remove – remove the item at the front of the queue
- Front – obtain the item at the front of the queue.

This can be used whenever a number of different items are waiting for the same resource, for example a printer may have a queue of print jobs waiting to be printed.

Tree

AQA M4
EDEXCEL M5
OCR M4
WJEC CP4

A binary tree has the format shown in Figure 11.

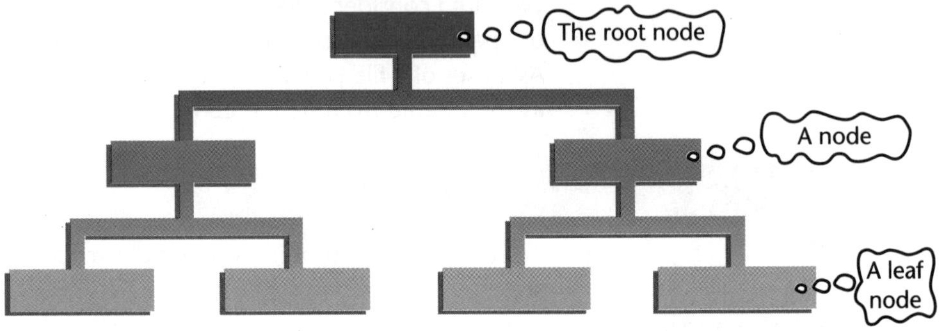

Figure 11

It is called a binary tree as each node has two sub-nodes (sometimes known as children). Typical operations on a binary tree are:

- Create – create a new tree
- Left – obtain the left sub-tree
- Right – obtain the right sub-tree
- Item – obtain the item at the root of the tree
- EmptyTree – discover whether the tree is empty.

Among the many uses of a binary tree, a compiler will normally hold arithmetic expressions in the form of a tree.

A special type of binary tree is the binary search tree. In this case, values are stored in sequence. The rule for a binary search tree is that the left sub-tree always holds values that come before the root and that the right sub-tree holds values that come after the root. Figure 12 shows an example.

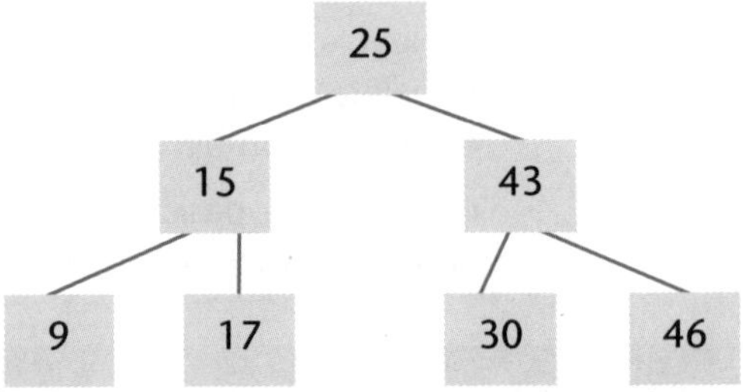

Figure 12

A binary search tree will normally have an operation insert that will add a new item in the correct place. This type of tree can be used to sort items by inserting them all into the tree and then retrieving them in order. It is very efficient to search for an item on a binary search tree so such trees are used to store reference data, for example the words in a dictionary.

> Data structures are defined by the operations that can be performed on them. The data structure can be defined without considering how it might be implemented.
>
> **KEY POINT**

Progress check

1 The names **Richards, Kerridge, Thompson, Hodges, Armstrong, Williams, Rogers** and **Leonard** are to be entered in the above order into a binary search tree.

The binary search is started below. Copy and complete the diagram.

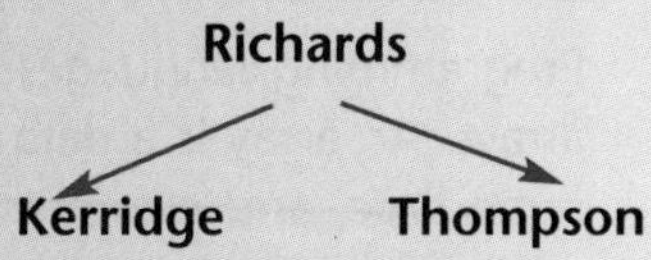

2 Give **one** reason for using binary tree structure rather than a linked list.

(a)

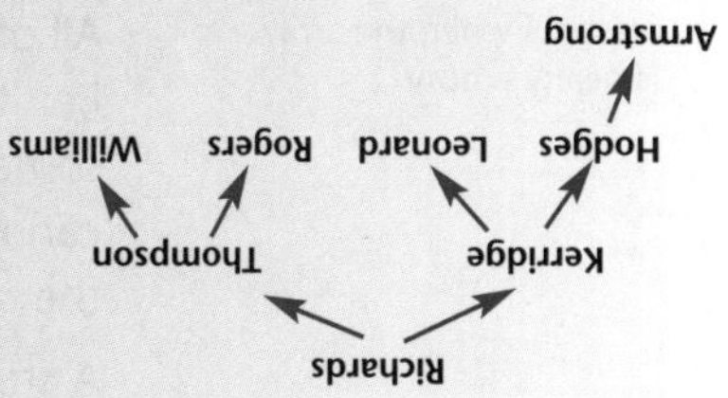

(b) An item can be found more quickly from a binary search tree.

3.3 Implementation of data structures

After studying this section you should be able to:

- *describe how data structures can be implemented*
- *explain the difference between static and dynamic implementation of data structures*
- *describe the terms 'pointer', 'free memory' and 'heap'*

LEARNING SUMMARY

Static implementation

AQA M4
OCR M4
WJEC CP4

An array can hold the data very efficiently if the array is full, but it is inflexible and very wasteful when the array is nearly empty.

Programming languages provide the facility to store collections of data items in arrays. An array is a data structure that contains a number of elements, all of the same type, and elements are accessed by subscripts. Arrays reside in contiguous areas of memory, i.e. an array will constitute a block of memory all in one place. Arrays are static, in that the memory is fixed in size. The number of items is specified when an array is declared and this does not change throughout the life of the program.

All of the above data structures can use an array as their means of implementation, i.e. it is possible to write the operations with the data items stored in an array. In some cases it is necessary to store additional information so that the data structure can remember where the first or last item is in the array or to remember which is the current item.

A stack might be implemented with an array to hold the items and an integer to remember the last item stored. An example stack that has had the items 5, 21 and 18 added might be as illustrated in Figure 13.

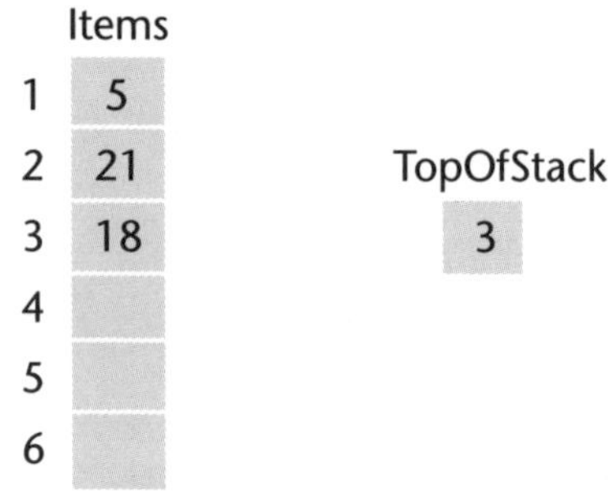

Figure 13

A queue that is implemented using an array will need two references: the front of the queue and the back of the queue. A queue has an additional problem. As items are added to the back of the queue and removed from the front, the queue will move down the array. When it reaches the bottom of the array the next item is placed at the top. In this way, the array acts as though it is in the form of a circle and we call this a circular array. A queue that has the values 56, 3, 12, 35 might be as shown in Figure 14.

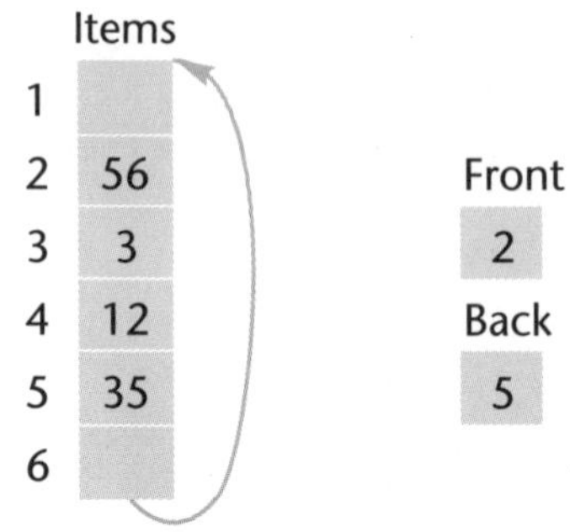

Figure 14

Figure 15 is an example of a binary tree.

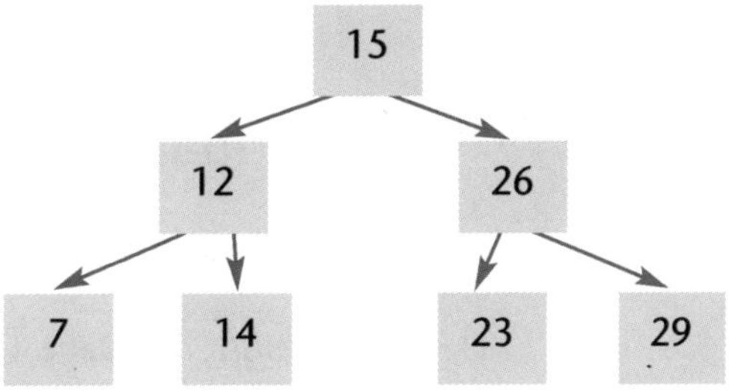

Figure 15

This binary tree can be implemented using an array as shown in Figure 16.

	Data	Left-pointer	Right-pointer
1	15	2	3
2	12	4	5
3	26	6	7
4	7	0	0
5	14	0	0
6	23	0	0
7	29	0	0

Figure 16

KEY POINT

This representation can be efficient if the amount of data is fairly constant but it is inflexible and it can be very wasteful when the amount of data is likely to change regularly. This is because the arrays have to be made large enough to take the maximum amount of expected data.

Dynamic implementation

AQA M4
OCR M4
WJEC CP4

A dynamic implementation will use more or less memory as required during the execution of the program. It obtains memory from the operating system as data are stored in the data structure. The operating system manages the memory of the computer and memory that is not being used by a program is called **free memory**. Free memory is stored in the **heap**. Free memory can be allocated to a program from the heap as the program is being executed. The program can release the memory when it has finished with it, in which case it is returned to the heap.

In order to implement dynamic data structures, pointers are used. A **pointer** is a variable that contains a number that represents an address. We say that the variable points to the memory. An example of a dynamic data structure is a linked list implemented as follows:

The pointers take up memory so this representation is not as efficient as the array representation, but it is much more flexible and generally wastes less memory.

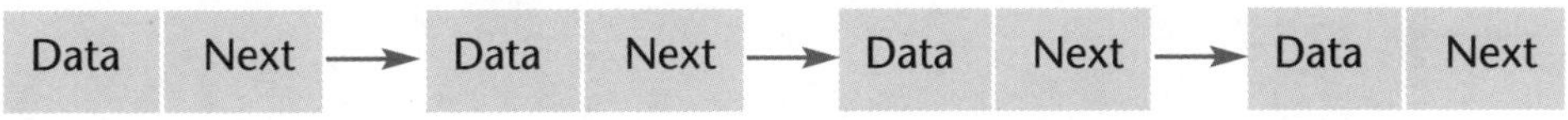

Data represents a data item that is to be stored and Next is a pointer to the next entry in the list.

Another example is a binary tree. In this case each node has two pointers, Left and Right (Figure 17).

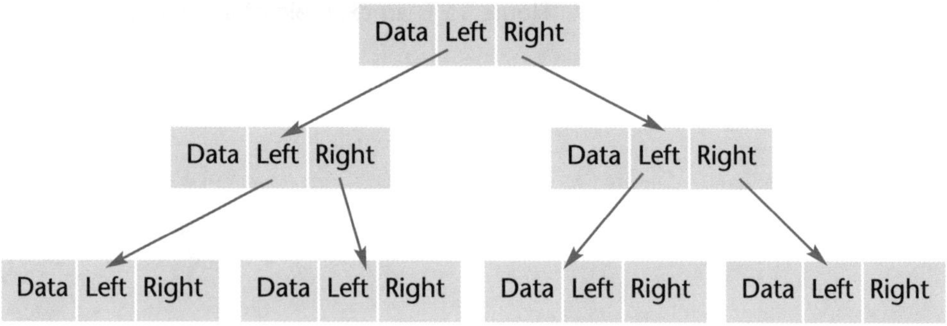

Figure 17

> The dynamic representation is more flexible. In a system where many data structures are present it is very easy to move items from one structure to another by manipulating pointers.
>
> **KEY POINT**

Progress check

Data is held in a linked list. The array *animals* contains records with the content shown.

Subscript	Data	Pointer
1	Elephant	
2	Deer	
3	Bear	
4	Rabbit	
5	Cow	
6		

(a) Give the values that would be needed in the pointer field of each non-empty record to produce a list in alphabetical order. A pointer value of 0 indicates the end of the list. [2]

(b) The variables *Start* and *Freestorage* are used to point to the start of the list and the next free space, respectively. What values should they contain? [2]

(c) Describe the steps needed to add 'Monkey' to the list. [5]

NEAB 2000, CP04

(a) Elephant 4
Deer 1
Bear 5
Rabbit 0
Cow 2

(b) Start = 3
Freestorage = 6

(c)
- Check for free space.
- Put 'Monkey' into the array at the position indicated by freestorage (animals[6]).
- Find the position where 'Monkey' must go in the list (between Elephant and Rabbit).
- Alter 'Elephant' pointer to point to 'Monkey'.
- Make 'Monkey' pointer point to 'Rabbit'.
- Alter the freestorage pointer to point to next space.

Sample questions and model answers

1

The algebraic expression

W * X – Y / Z

is stored as a binary tree in the three arrays: *item, leftpointer, rightpointer*, as shown in the table.

	Subscript						
	1	2	3	4	5	6	7
item	–	*	/	W	X	Y	Z
leftpointer	2	4	6	0	0	0	0
rightpointer	3	5	7	0	0	0	0

You could also obtain marks by stating that the data are held in a contiguous block of memory. Any two points will get you the marks.

(a) What is an array? [2]

(a) An array is a static data structure that contains elements that are all of the same type. Individual elements are accessed by subscripts.

(b) Draw a diagram of the binary tree represented by the three arrays: *item, leftpointer, rightpointer.*

It is not obvious where the root of the tree is but you can work it out as the '–' is the only item not to have a pointer referring to it.

(b)

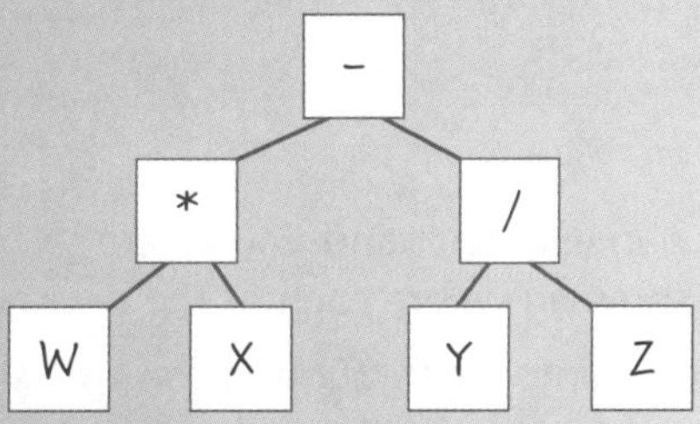

[5]

AEB 1998, Paper 2

2

(a) The names **Smith, Jala, Taylor, Avery, Hill, Brown, Ivor, Wang** and **Rigby** are to be entered in the above order into a binary tree structure. In each case, the left pointer indicates the condition

earlier in the alphabet

The tree structure is started below. Copy and complete the diagram. You can use just the initial letter of each name if you wish: **S, J, T, A, H, B, I, W** and **R**. [4]

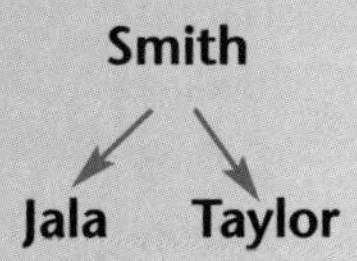

[4]

The important point here is that the question stated which order the items were to be entered. If you follow that order you should have no problem.

(a)

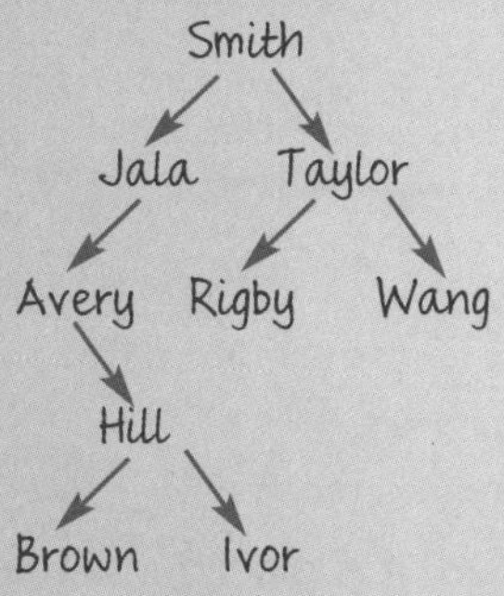

This is because you would have to work through the list from the beginning.

(b) (i) Give **one** advantage of a binary tree structure over a linear linked list. [1]

(b) (i) It is normally possible to find an entry much more quickly.

(ii) Give **one** advantage of a linear linked over a binary tree structure.

Another possible answer is: 'There are additional pointers that have to be stored'.

(ii) Either – The programming is generally less complex than for a binary tree or – There are additional program overheads for a binary tree.

Practice examination questions

1 A binary tree is used to represent the following names in alphabetical order:

Elizabeth, John, Mary, Abdul, Yacub

(a) Draw a diagram of the binary tree with Elizabeth at the root node. [2]

(b) Show how your binary tree might be represented using one or more arrays. [2]

NEAB 1998, CP04

2 (a) The *binary tree* is a type of data structure. State **two** other examples of data structures other than the binary tree. [2]

(b) The following binary tree contains a number of surnames.

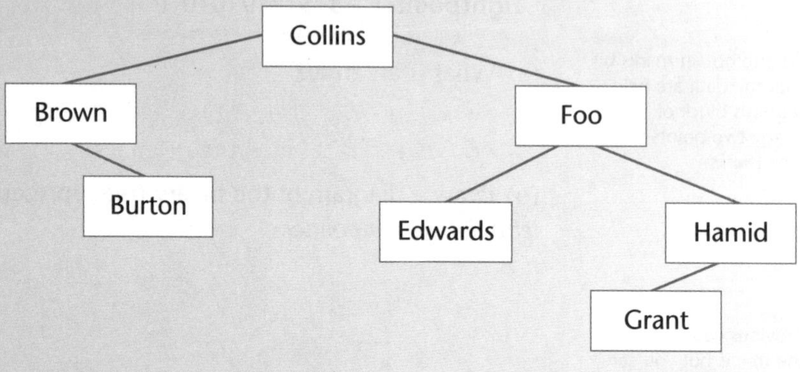

(i) Two new names, *Carter* and *Cooper* are to be added in that order. Copy the diagram, showing where each of the new names will be inserted. [2]

(ii) In a particular implementation of this tree structure, arrays are used, where each name has a *left-pointer* and a *right-pointer*, pointing to another element in the tree.

The array for the original tree above is shown below: a record is kept of the root of the tree and the first free space, as shown:

	array element	name	left-pointer	right-pointer
	1	Foo	3	2
	2	Hamid	7	0
	3	Edwards	0	0
root →	4	Collins	5	1
	5	Brown	0	8
free →	6		9	
	7	Grant	0	0
	8	Burton	0	0
	9		10	
	10		11	
	..			
	..			

As a new name is added, it is placed in a free location and the two pointers are adjusted as necessary.

When the name *Carter* is added, the contents of some rows of the above array will change. Copy and amend the relevant rows, to show what the changes will be. (Do not repeat for Cooper.) [2]

WJEC 2000, C4

Chapter 4

Operating systems

The following topics are covered in this chapter:

- *Operating system fundamentals*
- *Process management*
- *Memory management*
- *Input/output management*

4.1 Operating system fundamentals

LEARNING SUMMARY

After studying this section you should be able to:

- *explain the purpose of an operating system*
- *describe the role of job control language*
- *select appropriate user interfaces*
- *explain what is meant by spooling*
- *describe what is meant by dynamically linked libraries (DLLs)*
- *explain the accountancy and security features of an operating system*

Operating system features

EDEXCEL	M4
EDEXCEL	M4
OCR	M4
WJEC	CP5

The operating system also makes it straightforward for the user to make efficient use of the resources of the computer system.

An operating system consists of a number of programs that together make efficient use of the hardware of the computer system. A typical operating system will have the following parts.

- Kernel – this program forms the heart of the operating system.
- Device drivers – these small programs are provided to control the various peripheral devices.
- User interface – this program provides the human/computer interface (HCI).
- System programs – various programs that provide services for the user, e.g. a disk formatter.

There may well be a choice of user interfaces and they will normally be configurable to provide the 'look and feel' that the user requires. In order that settings can be reproduced they are often placed in a configuration file (also called a start-up file or a boot file) that is read when the system is started up.

Spooling

The spool program is commonly used to control the output to a printer. When data are to be printed they are passed to the spooler as a print job. The spooler stores the print job on the spool-file before passing it to the printer. In this way the spool-file contains a queue of print jobs waiting to be printed. This program allows several programs to print to the same printer. It ensures that a print job will be printed as a continuous printout without being affected by other programs. It is especially useful on a network where many users can use the same printer.

A spooler will often operate in the background, i.e. it will allow a user to continue with other work while printing is going on.

KEY POINT

Spooling allows the use of a printer by many programs or many users at the same time.

Key points from AS

- **Operating systems**
  Revise AS pages 54–57

Programs stored in a library may be as short as a routine to clear the screen.

Libraries

As the operating system consists of many small programs they are normally stored on magnetic disk in the form of libraries. A library is simply a file containing many programs. A program is loaded into memory from a library by a program known as a loader.

There are two types of loader:

- absolute loaders
- relocating loaders.

An absolute loader loads the program into a fixed part of memory. The start address of such a program is naturally fixed.

It is often convenient for the operating system to be able to load a program from a library into any part of the computer's memory that is available. A relocating loader achieves this. The program must be stored in such a way that this is possible and a library containing this type of program is known as a dynamically linked library (DLL). All addresses in such a program will be stored as displacements from the start of the program and the start address will be stored in a register. All actual addresses will be computed using base register addressing (Figure 18).

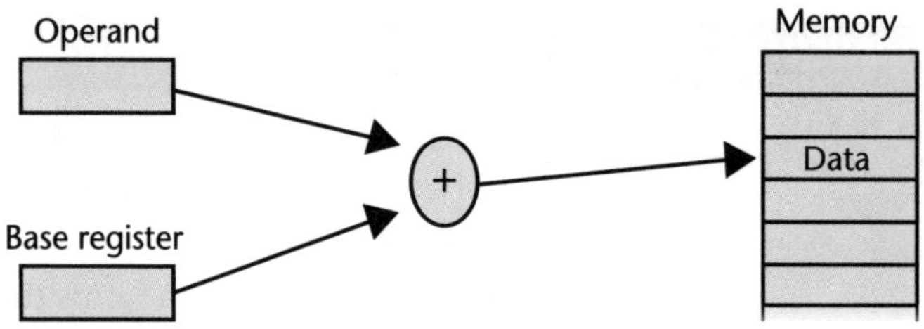

Figure 18

> DLLs can be loaded into any location in the memory.
>
> KEY POINT

Accountancy

An operating system will have some accountancy features that provide information about the use of the computer system. Typical information that might be available is:

- the amount of disk space allocated to each user
- the amount of disk space used by each user
- the amount of time a program uses the processor
- the amount of memory used by a program
- the amount of time a user is online.

Charging may be by the resources used, e.g. disk space, or the amount of time, e.g. logon time.

This information can be used to charge for the use of the computer system.

> The operating system is able to compute appropriate charges to be made to each user.
>
> KEY POINT

Security

An operating system will provide security features to protect the data that are stored on the computer system. Typical features are:

- passwords to log on to the system
- different levels of users
- passwords to access individual files or directories
- encryption of data
- access controls to files (Read, Write, Execute, Append, etc.)
- memory protection to prevent users from straying into others' memory.

It is possible to have levels of password, and different types of user will have different access rights.

In this way a user, or a program, can be allocated certain resources and the operating system will provide a secure environment. The operating system can protect the computer system from external risks such as hackers and competitors. It can also protect the users from each other.

KEY POINT

The operating system can make every part of the computer system secure.

Progress check

An operating system provides Read, Write, Delete, Execute and Append access controls to files. Which access controls would you expect to be enabled on the following files?

1 A program that forms part of the operating system.
2 A document that you have just written.
3 A file to log the transactions of an online system.
4 A bank account file that is online to customers. [4]

You need to think carefully about what rights are definitely required, and not allow any that are not needed.

1 Execute
2 Read, Write, Append, Delete
3 Append
4 Read

4.2 Process management

LEARNING SUMMARY

After studying this section you should be able to:

- *describe the principles of multiprogramming*
- *describe how the operating system manages multiprogramming*
- *describe scheduling strategies*
- *describe systems that combine batch and interactive modes*

Process management tools

AQA	M4
EDEXCEL	M4
OCR	M4
WJEC	CP5

Multiprogramming

When a program is being executed we call it a process. If we follow the progress of a process we notice that most program instructions are executed in quick succession by the processor. There are some instructions that involve the use of a peripheral, for example a disk, tape, keyboard, printer, etc. When a peripheral operation is performed the process has to wait as the peripherals operate at a much slower speed. The life cycle of a single process is illustrated in Figure 19.

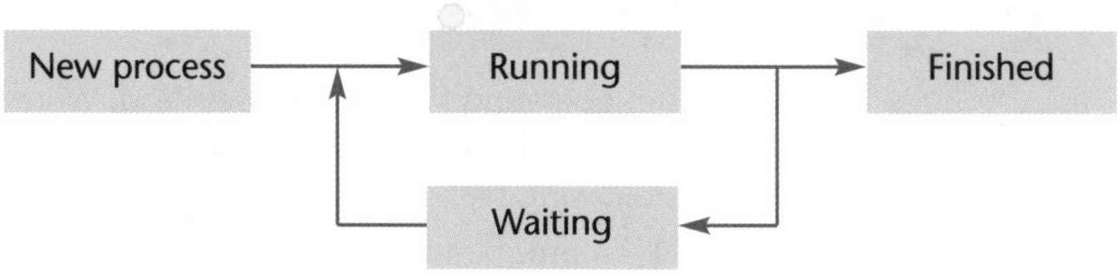

Figure 19

One process can execute while the others are waiting. It appears that the processes are all being executed at the same time.

When a process is waiting the processor is available to execute another process. As the waiting time for a process is usually much longer than the time the process is running it is possible to have a number of processes in this cycle at the same time.

The operating system can manage this by maintaining two queues of processes: a queue of processes that are waiting and a queue of processes that are ready to run (Figure 20).

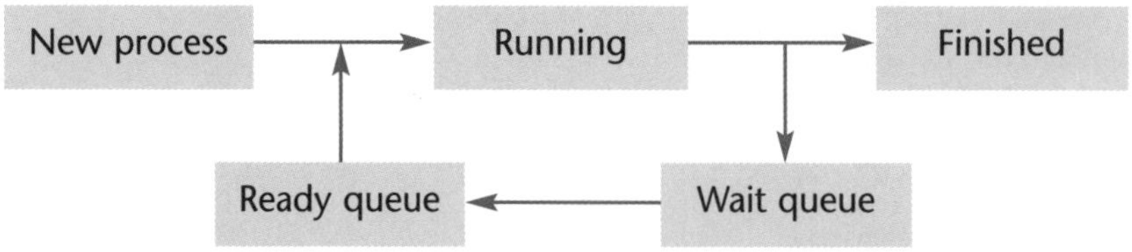

Figure 20

Note that the interrupt is generated when the input/output operation is **completed**.

The peripherals operate in such a way that the operating system issues a command to the peripheral to perform a data transfer (for example, transfer a block of data from a disk to a buffer) and the peripheral generates an interrupt when the transfer is completed. When an interrupt is generated the operating system moves a process from the wait queue to the ready queue.

Key points from AS

- **Resource management**
  Revise AS page 55

Process control block

Each process has a process control block (PCB) that contains its current state. Figure 21 shows some of the contents typically included in a PCB.

Process ID239845	
Owner ID	W.Butcher
Priority	27
Status	WAITING
Units of processor time used	264
Resource waiting for	Disk5
Link to another PCB	Next PCB in WAIT Q
Registers	Contents of Registers when the process last stopped running

Figure 21

When a process stops running, its current state must be saved so that it can be restarted later. The PCB contains space to store all the registers when a process ceases to occupy the processor and joins the wait queue. These can be reloaded from the PCB when the process returns to a running state. The wait queue and the ready queue are both implemented in the form of linked lists so each PCB will contain a link to another PCB. This makes it very easy to move a PCB from one queue to another by simply changing some links.

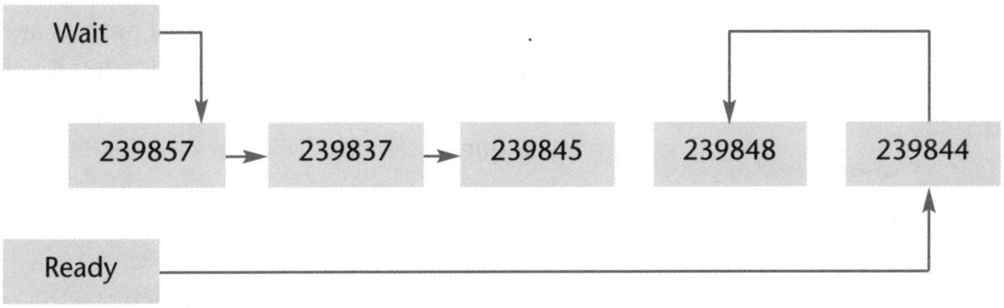

Figure 22

In Figure 22, process 239845 is in the wait queue. When the disk transfer is complete it will be moved to the ready queue and the situation will now be as shown in Figure 23.

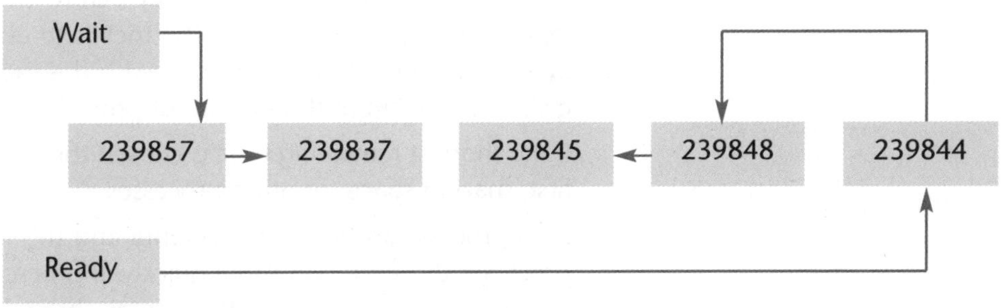

Figure 23

So the process has been moved from one queue to another by changing two links.

> The state of any process is contained in its process control block.
>
> KEY POINT

Scheduling strategies

When multiprogramming is taking place the operating system can adopt various strategies for taking processes off the ready queue and allowing them to run. They include:

Different strategies are used in different circumstances. It depends on the requirements of the individual system.

- process the maximum number of jobs
- be as fair to each user as possible
- provide acceptable response time to online users
- keep all devices as busy as possible
- as the system becomes overloaded, attempt to degrade steadily rather than suddenly collapse altogether
- avoid deadlock.

Often the online processes are placed on a ready queue separate from the batch processes. Batch processes are taken from the batch queue only when the online queue is empty.

The job of scheduling is often divided into three tasks:

- long-term scheduling
- medium-term scheduling
- short-term scheduling.

The long-term scheduler will organise a queue of batch jobs that are yet to be started. When space becomes available this scheduler will select an appropriate job.

The medium-term scheduler will monitor the process of multiprogramming. If it detects that there are too many processes attempting to use the processor it has the power to temporarily suspend a process and take it out of the processing loop. When the system is no longer overloaded it will allow the process to continue.

The short-term scheduler is the program that will select the next process from the ready queue.

Scheduling algorithms

Various algorithms can be used to achieve the required strategy. Typical algorithms include:

- shortest burst time
- shortest remaining time
- priority scheduling
- round robin.

A burst is the time spent running before the process will have to wait for an input/output (I/O) operation. The trick is to estimate how long the next burst will be for each process. If the process with the shortest next burst time is chosen, this gives the maximum throughput of processes.

If the shortest remaining time is chosen then the shortest processes will be finished first, making space for other processes.

Each process can be given a priority and this allows some control to push certain processes through the system quickly. If processes that have a large amount of I/O are given a high priority then total throughput will be maximised. If online processes are given a high priority then this will give rapid response to these users.

It is possible to limit the time that each process is allowed to run before it is removed and placed back in the ready queue: we have a situation that is sometimes known as a timeslice system. By using a first in first out (FIFO) ready queue each process is executed for a short time in turn. This method is known as round robin.

> There are many scheduling algorithms. Each method is appropriate for a particular situation.
>
> KEY POINT

Deadlock

When several processes are attempting to use a number of resources it is possible for a situation known as deadlock to develop. Deadlock occurs as follows. Process A opens a file and then attempts to use the printer. Unfortunately process B is already using the printer so process A has to wait. Process B subsequently attempts to open the same file that process A is already using. We now have a situation where neither process can proceed (Figure 24).

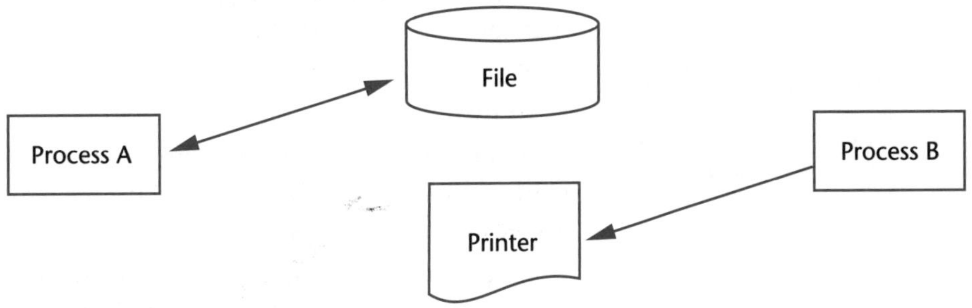

Figure 24

The two approaches are to attempt to prevent deadlock or to try to recover after it has occurred.

There are various strategies to deal with deadlock.

- Do not allow a process to start until all its resources are available.
- Always allocate resources in the same sequence.
- When deadlock occurs, allow the operating system to remove a process.

Threads

It is possible to have separate threads of execution within a process. An example might be a word-processor that is used on a multi-user system where several users can be processing their own documents concurrently. They can all use a single copy of the word-processor program that will be in the memory of the computer. There will be a single word-processing program but each user will have a separate thread of execution.

Progress check

In a batch multiprogramming environment, the following three programs are ready and waiting to run:

a payroll program
a complicated scientific calculation
the printing of a long queue of reports.

1 Explain **one** reason why the queue of reports would be allocated the highest priority. [2]

2 Explain **one** reason why the scientific calculation would be given the lowest priority. [2]

AEB 1998, Paper 2

1 The long queue of print jobs will be highly I/O bound so it will only need the processor for short bursts. In between bursts the processor will be free to perform other tasks.
2 The scientific calculation will be highly processor bound so it will stop other processes from using the processor.

4.3 Memory management

After studying this section you should be able to:

LEARNING SUMMARY

- *explain what is meant by partitioned memory*
- *explain what is meant by virtual memory*

Methods of memory management

AQA	M4
EDEXCEL	M4
OCR	M4
WJEC	CP5

Key points from AS

- **Resource management** *Revise AS page 55*

Partitioned memory

The memory manager organises memory into partitions to make it easier to manage. Partitions may be one of two types:

- pages
- segments.

Pages are fairly small (typically the size of a disk sector) and are used to implement virtual memory (see below). Segments are large areas of memory that are used for a specific purpose. Typical segments are:

- code segment – used to store the program (this may well be read only)
- data segment – used to store the data variables
- stack segment – used to implement a system stack.

Some systems have segments that are fixed in size. This can be a disadvantage as memory is wasted if they are not full.

Virtual memory

A computer system can only execute programs and process data when they are placed in the computer's memory. This places a limit on the number of programs that can be multiprogrammed to the number that can be stored in the memory. An operating system can allow extra programs to be multiprogrammed by implementing virtual memory. An area of the computer's hard disk is allocated to the virtual memory (Figure 25).

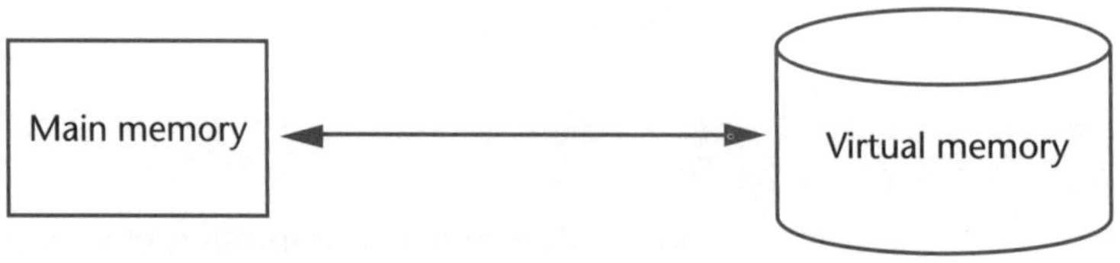

Figure 25

The virtual memory area is divided into pages and the contents of the pages are brought into the computer's main memory as they are required. A virtual memory address consists of a page number and an offset within the page (Figure 26). To implement virtual memory addresses a page table is used. A page table contains the start address of each page that is in the computer's memory.

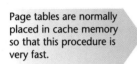

Page tables are normally placed in cache memory so that this procedure is very fast.

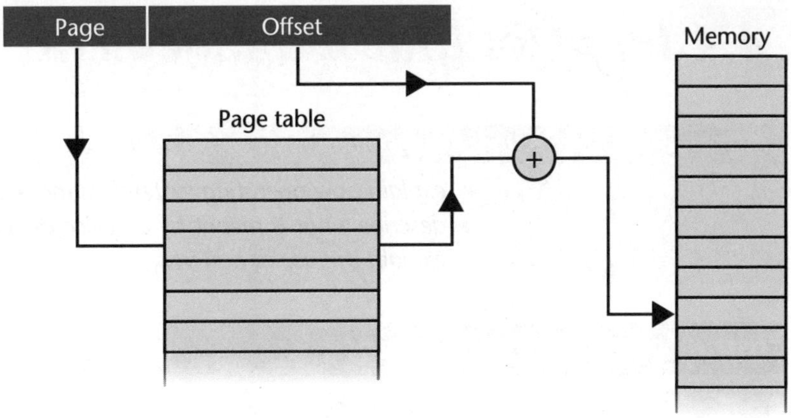

Figure 26

When disk thrashing is occurring an improvement in performance can be achieved by installing additional memory.

The page table also contains a bit that indicates whether the page is currently in memory. If it is not in memory the operating system will have to copy the page from the disk to the memory before proceeding. This will normally involve overwriting an existing page in the memory. If there is insufficient main memory this will happen frequently, causing slow execution of the programs. When this happens we say that disk thrashing is taking place.

> Virtual memory allows more programs to be executed concurrently.
>
> KEY POINT

Progress check

Explain why the installation of additional memory might improve the performance of a computer system. [5]

If there is limited main memory and the operating system is implementing virtual memory, disk thrashing may be taking place. This is due to the large number of page replacements that are occurring. Increasing the amount of main memory will allow more pages to be in memory at any time. This will reduce the number of times the disk is accessed and will therefore improve the performance of the computer system.

An additional point to make is that disks transfer data much more slowly than memory.

4.4 Input/output management

After studying this section you should be able to:

- *explain how operating systems manage file space*
- *describe what is meant by a device driver*
- *explain the use of buffers*

LEARNING SUMMARY

Input/output management

AQA	M4
EDEXCEL	M4
OCR	M4
WJEC	CP5

File management

The file manager part of the operating system will normally implement a hierarchical directory structure like that illustrated in Figure 27.

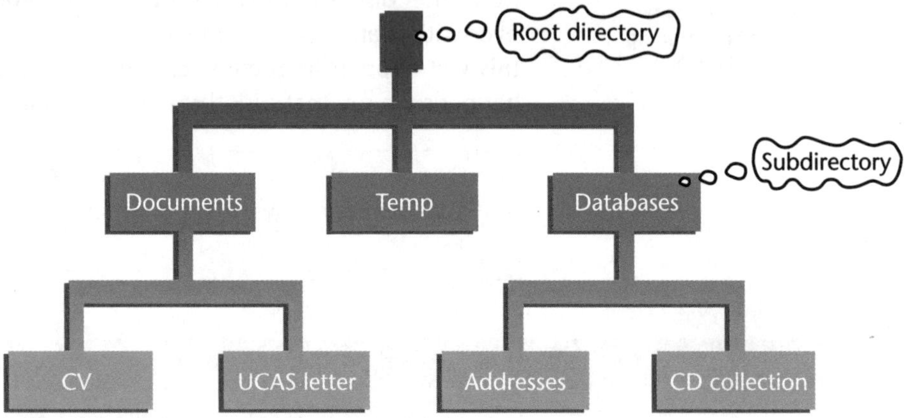

Figure 27

Each directory or file may be given access rights. Examples are:

- Read
- Write
- Delete
- Execute
- Append.

These rights may be allocated to a single user or a group of users. In this way files and/or directories may be hidden from users. Users may be unable to change files even when they can view them. In addition it is possible to place passwords on directories and/or files.

Each user will have an individual set of access rights.

When several users are able to update the same file this can cause problems if they attempt to change the same data concurrently, for example in an airline booking system. To solve this problem the operating system may be able to lock files or individual records. When a user locks a file it is not possible for another user to access that file.

Disk organisation

A disk is organised into tracks and sectors. Some tracks and sectors are used for specific purposes. One sector is called the boot sector and is used to hold an initial bootstrap program to enable the operating system to be loaded when the computer is turned on. Typically, one or two tracks are allocated to the directory of the disk. The files may be organised in various ways. The simplest method is to store each file in a contiguous area (i.e. the file is stored in adjacent sectors). In this case the directory will contain the name of each file, the start sector and the length (Figure 28).

Key points from AS

- **File management**
  Revise AS page 55

Name	***Directory Start***	***Length***
FRED.DOC	0	2
EX1.CPP	14	3
MAIL.DOC	19	6
MAN.TXT	28	4
PIC1.BMP	6	2

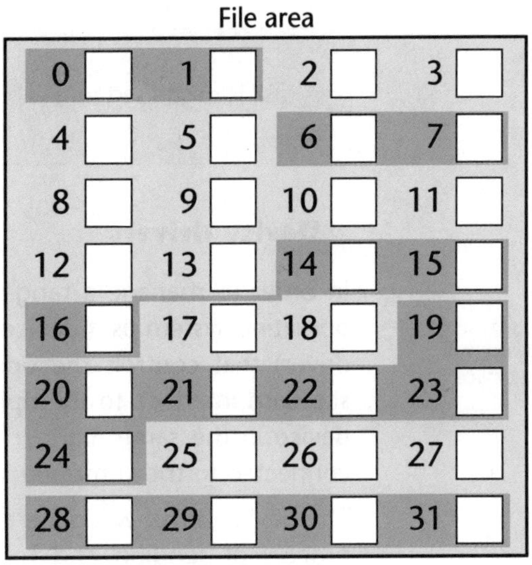

Figure 28

This approach has the problem that new files cannot be inserted into the gaps that occur when old files are deleted. As the operating system does not know how big a file is when it is being created it cannot be fitted into an empty space in the file area. Most modern systems use a linked file system that implements each file as a linked list. This allows files to be placed in any empty sectors on the disk wherever they are. This method often uses a **file allocation table** (FAT) that has an entry for each **cluster** on the disk. A cluster comprises one or more sectors.

Suppose that we have a file stored in clusters 9, 16, 1, 10, 25. There will be a file allocation table like that in Figure 29.

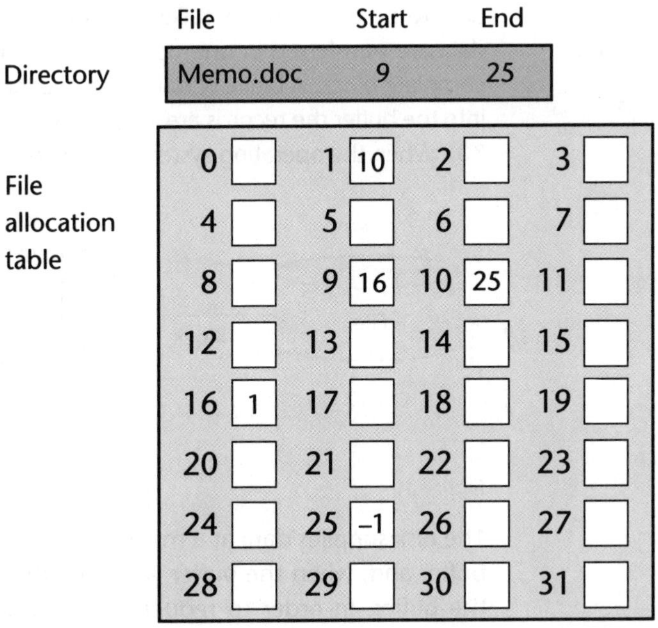

The entry –1 is used to indicate the end of the file. This should agree with the end of file cluster in the directory entry.

Figure 29

The first files to be stored on the disk will be placed in contiguous areas. As files are deleted, gaps appear on the disk and subsequent files are placed in the gaps. This causes a file to be placed in small separate areas rather than in one contiguous area. When this happens the file is said to be **fragmented**. Fragmented files take longer to read from the disk as the heads have to move more frequently and this also causes extra wear and tear on the mechanism. To solve this problem the operating system will normally have a system program that reorganises the files into contiguous areas (often called a defragmenter).

> A disk is organised into a boot sector, a directory and a data area.
>
> KEY POINT

Device driver

Each type of device will require its own device driver.

In order to manage a range of I/O devices (keyboard, printer, mouse, etc.) the operating system uses device drivers. Each device has a small program (the device driver) that controls the operations of one type of device and also provides a standard interface to the operating system. The operating system can treat each device in the same manner and yet it can allow a wide range of devices to be connected to the computer system.

The device driver will generate the appropriate signals to operate the device. The process of sending and receiving signals to/from another device in order to communicate is called handshaking. An example might be a computer system that is attempting to send some data to a printer. The device would send a signal to say 'are you ready to receive?'. The printer will reply with a signal to say 'yes' or 'no'.

> Device drivers allow a range of devices to be connected to a computer system.
>
> KEY POINT

Buffers

The memory operates at a much higher speed than the peripheral.

When data are transferred from a device, the part of the memory that will hold the data to be transferred is called a buffer. In the case of a disk or tape where blocks of data are transferred in one operation, the buffer has to be large enough to hold the complete block. A block of data usually contains several records. After the block is read into the buffer the records are supplied to the program by the operating system (Figure 30). When the operating system comes to the end of the buffer it reads the next block.

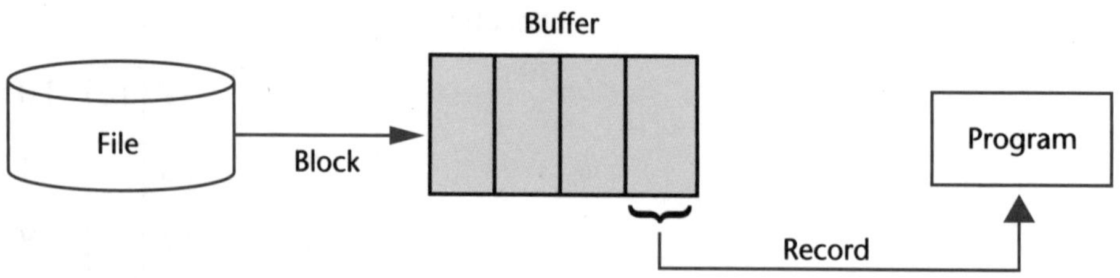

Figure 30

The disk supplies data at a much slower rate than the program can read it from the buffer and, when the buffer is empty, the program has to wait for the disk to refill the buffer. In order to reduce the waiting time, double buffering is often used. Double buffering uses two buffers and the disk can be filling one buffer while the program is removing records from the other (Figure 31).

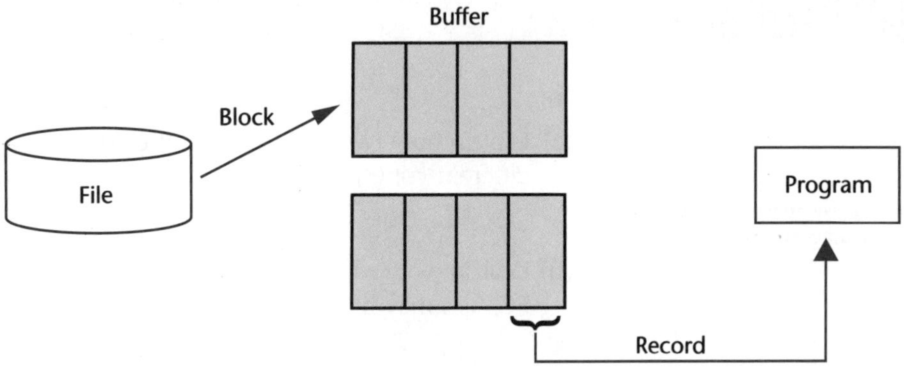

Figure 31

This technique can be equally applied to the output of data.

Disk cache is particularly effective when a database is stored on a disk.

This idea can be extended by providing disk drives with additional memory, called disk cache, that is used to store blocks of data. Data are transferred into cache memory whenever they are read or written to the disk. It is often the case that data that have been read once are required again within a short space of time. If they are still in the cache then the process is speeded up. The cache will also contain the disk directory and any other indexes as these are used regularly.

KEY POINT

The buffer allows devices of various different speeds to be connected to the computer system.

Progress check

When a program is being loaded the operating system detects that there is a problem with the FAT.

1 How can the operating system detect that the FAT is corrupt? [3]

2 Give two ways the FAT might become corrupt. [2]

1 The operating system can follow the links through the FAT to the end of the file. If the end of the file does not agree with the final cluster stored in the directory entry for the file the FAT is corrupt.

2 Hardware failure might cause the FAT to become corrupt.
Power failure (or simply turning the system off) at an inappropriate moment might cause the FAT to become corrupt.

Sample questions and model answers

1

(a) Explain how two PCs, running the same operating system, can start up with different configurations. [2]

(a) Start-up commands are placed in a boot file.

An equally good answer would be an autoexec file.

(b) Explain why, when loading a new applications package onto the hard disk of a PC, files may become fragmented. [2]

(b) Initially all files are contiguous but when files are deleted gaps are created on the disk. New files are loaded into the gaps and so they may become fragmented.

(c) Explain how the operating system can load a file that is fragmented on a disk. [5]

(c) Files are stored in distinct clusters and the file allocation table (FAT) records how files are stored. The directory entry will point to the FAT entry for the 1st cluster in the file. The 1st cluster entry in the FAT will point to the second cluster. The 2nd cluster entry will point to the 3rd cluster and so on. The last cluster contains an end of file code.

(d) A PC user has created a number of very large files which are to be printed. Explain how a print spooler is used to handle these jobs while the user continues to use the PC for other tasks. [6]

(d) The spooler is a program that maintains a spool file. The spool file contains a queue of jobs that need to be printed. As jobs come to the front of the queue the spooler sends them to the printer. The spooler sends a batch of data to the printer and then relinquishes the processor. When the printer has finished the batch of data it interrupts the processor and the spooler is restarted.

Note that there are six marks here so a reasonably full description is required.

OCR specimen 2509

2

A process can be classified as I/O bound (input/output bound) if it collects large volumes of input and/or produces considerable quantities of output. Similarly a process consisting mainly of calculations/computations (using CPU/memory) can be classified as processor-bound.

Explain which type of process should be given higher priority in a multiprogramming environment to ensure efficient use of the resources available. [2]

The I/O-bound process should be given higher priority as it will quickly release the processor and allow the processor-bound process to continue.

This is an important point to remember. Jobs with short bursts of processor activity should be given top priority.

NEAB 1999, CP05

Practice examination questions

1 Disk directories record information about the files that are stored on disk. State three items of information that, typically, would be recorded. [3]

AEB 1997, Paper 2

2 Explain the term *virtual memory*. [4]

AEB 1997, Paper 2

3 A method of increasing the flow of large amounts of data from a disk drive is to use a disk cache. What is disk cache and how does its use speed up the flow of data? [3]

NEAB 2000, CP05

4 (a) A multiprogramming (multitasking) operating system allocates resources to programs as they require them. Explain how *deadlock* can arise between programs using this type of operating system. [2]

(b) A different multiprogramming (multitasking) operating system will only allow a program to be loaded if all the resources it needs are available. At the start of a session the following peripherals are available for use:

5 disk drives
3 printers.

The amount of memory available for use by new programs is 10 Mb.

The priority of the programs waiting to start and the peripherals and memory they require are shown below. (Priority 1 is the highest.)

Program	A	B	C	D	E
Priority	1	2	3	4	5
Disk drives	3	3	1	1	1
Printers	1	1	1	1	1
Memory	3500K	4000K	3000K	4500K	2000K

(i) Explain which programs will be loaded initially, assuming program priority takes precedence over other considerations. For the remaining programs explain why they have not been loaded. [5]

(ii) Once the programs have started running, what has to happen to allow one of the remaining programs to be loaded? [1]

(iii) For each possible way this could happen, which of the remaining programs will be selected? [3]

NEAB 2000, CP05

5 Using a diagram, explain how double buffering is used to speed up the flow of data. [3]

NEAB 1998, CP05

6 (a) Within a multiprogramming environment a process can be in one of three different basic states. Briefly describe each of these basic states. [3]

(b) (i) State the principles by which priorities are allocated to programs in a multiprogramming environment. [2]

(ii) How do these principles ensure efficient use of the processor and other resources? [2]

NEAB 1998, CP05

Chapter 5

Files and databases

The following topics are covered in this chapter:

- *Indexed sequential files*
- *Random files*
- *Relational databases*

5.1 Indexed sequential files

After studying this section you should be able to:

- *describe indexed sequential files*
- *explain the management of overflow*
- *describe housekeeping*
- *explain the use of multilevel indexes*

LEARNING SUMMARY

Organisation of an indexed sequential file

EDEXCEL M4
WJEC CP5

An indexed sequential file consists of three parts:

- the index
- the home area
- the overflow area.

As the home area is in sequence, this type of file can be accessed sequentially. It can also be accessed randomly through the index.

The Index

The index contains record keys and disk addresses. The record key must be one or more fields that together identify an individual record; that is, no two records can have the same key. Associated with each record key there will be a disk address (surface, track and sector number) to identify a specific sector of the home area (Figure 32). The home area will contain the data records stored in record key sequence.

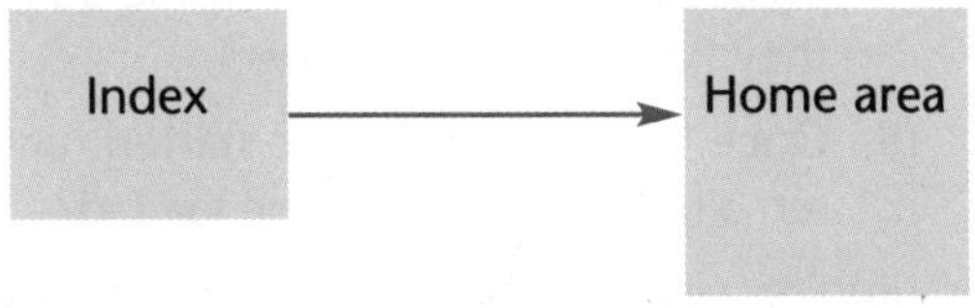

Figure 32

Home area

The sequential file is normally organised into blocks that contain several records (a block may consist of one or more sectors of the disk). It is normal practice to partially fill these blocks when the file is created to allow additional records to be inserted. If we assume that a block can contain ten records, we might choose to store seven records in each block, allowing space for three additional records to be inserted into a block during the processing of the file (Figure 33 shows an example). In this case we say that we have a packing density of 70%.

Home area

Able	Binns	Box	Briggs	Bright	Brown	Childs			
Clark	Cox	Dance	Double	Draper	Evans	Fal			
Fox	Frans	George	King	Kong	Ling	Lion			
Mok	Nixon	Oxford	Rogers	Stewart	Thomas	Walker			

Figure 33

Key points from AS

- **Files**
  Revise AS pages 80–82

When records are stored in overflow this will slow down the subsequent processing of the file.

Overflow

As the file is processed, records may be added to the file. As each home block has some space, the records can normally be added to the home area. The overflow area is provided to place records that will not fit into their correct block in the home area. When this happens, a pointer is placed in the home area to indicate the position in the overflow area of any additional records (Figure 34).

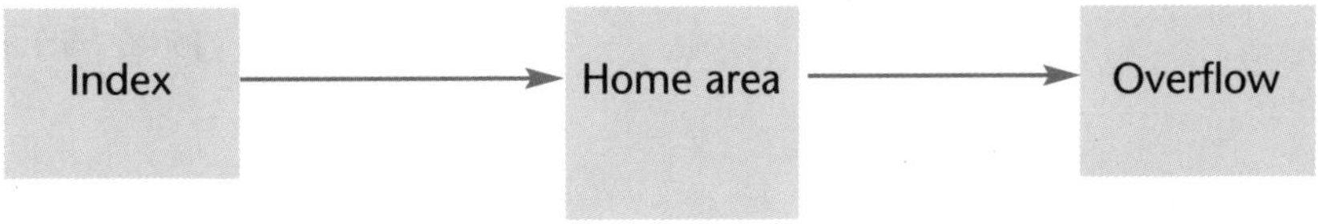

Figure 34

Housekeeping

As the file is processed, new records are added and old records are deleted. When a new record is added, it is added to the home area if there is space or to the overflow area if the home block is full. When a record is deleted the record is marked as deleted but the record is not removed from the file. Throughout all this processing *the indexes will not be updated.*

Let us consider a file that has four records to a block and the packing density is 75%. When the file is created a home block might have the data shown in Figure 35.

Block 7	Key	Name	Home no.	Mobile
	2837	Norman Louisa	02083889345	07801123123
	2840	Harrison Henry	01206834921	07710994504
	2893	Miller Sarah	01473283674	07806736188
Overflow block				

Figure 35

A new record is to be added with a key of 2867. It must be placed in this block (Figure 36).

Block 7	Key	Name	Home no.	Mobile
	2837	Norman Louisa	02083889345	07801123123
	2840	Harrison Henry	01206834921	07710994504
	2893	Miller Sarah	01473283674	07806736188
	2867	Bateman Kevin	01672889300	07808543946
Overflow block				

Figure 36

Another record is to be added. This record has the key 2888. As there is no room in block 7 the new record will have to be placed in an overflow block, say block 92 (Figure 37).

Block 7	Key	Name	Home no.	Mobile
	2837	Norman Louisa	02083889345	07801123123
	2840	Harrison Henry	01206834921	07710994504
	2893	Miller Sarah	01473283674	07806736188
	2867	Bateman Kevin	01672889300	07808543946
Overflow block	92			

Block 92	Key	Name	Home no.	Mobile
	2888	Jones Michael	02074671183	07805227635
Overflow block				

Figure 37

The time between reorganisations depends on the amount of updating that is going on.

As processing continues the home area becomes more and more disorganised and many records are placed in the overflow area. The effect is to increase the time taken to access the file. To solve this problem the file is regularly reorganised using a housekeeping program. The housekeeping program tidies up the file by placing all the records into the home area and rewriting the index. It does this by reading the file sequentially and writing the data on to a new file.

Indexes

Some files use the smallest key in each block rather than the largest. Either will work.

A typical index entry will contain the address of the block (or cylinder) and the largest key to be stored in that block. An example is shown in Figure 38.

Block number	Largest key
1	4957
2	5015
3	5022
4	5038
5	5050

Figure 38

If the file is very large there may be more than two levels of index.

If an indexed sequential file is large, the index may be organised into a cylinder index and, for each cylinder, a block index. The cylinder will have an entry for each cylinder and the block index will contain an entry for each block in the cylinder. Having two levels of index allows faster access when the index is large.

Progress check

1 An indexed sequential file has been created with a packing density of 80%.

(a) Explain what is meant by a packing density of 80% when applied to an indexed sequential file.

(b) Why is the packing density less than 100%?

2 After the indexed sequential file has been updated it is noticed that the file is taking longer to process.

(a) Explain what is likely to be slowing down the processing of the file.

(b) Describe how the problem can be solved.

1 (a) Data are only being stored in 80% of each block in the home area.
(b) To allow for the insertion of additional records.

2 (a) Records have been placed in the overflow area. After reading the index it takes a single disk access to read a record in the home area. Each time the overflow area is accessed it takes at least two disk accesses: one to read the home area and one to read the overflow.
(b) The solution is solved by reorganising the file using a housekeeping program. This program will copy the file to a new file, placing all the overflow records into the home area and rewriting the indexes.

5.2 Random files

After studying this section you should be able to:

- describe a random file structure
- describe hashing algorithms
- explain the management of overflow

LEARNING SUMMARY

Structure of a random file

EDEXCEL M4
WJEC CP5

Structure of a random file

A random file is used for direct access only.

A random file, like an indexed sequential file, also stores the records in blocks. The records are not stored in sequence: the position of a record is determined by a hashing algorithm. When a record is to be stored in the file a hashing algorithm is applied to the record key and this determines the block that is to be used. The blocks are numbered giving a range of block numbers, for example a file containing 500 blocks might be numbered 0 to 499, and the hash algorithm will generate a number within this range. A simple hash algorithm for a 1000-block file might be to take the last three digits of a numerical record key (Figure 39).

Record key	Block
2993847	847
5929758	758
4446789	789
3982281	281

Figure 39

This will give a value between 000 and 999 and will operate successfully on a 1000-block file. Hash algorithms can be very sophisticated and perform quite complex calculations in an attempt to spread the records throughout the file.

When records are deleted they are marked as deleted but they are not removed from the file. After processing the file there may be a number of these deleted records taking up space and slowing down the processing of the file. When this happens it is necessary to reorganise the file by copying the data on to a new file, removing the deleted records.

Overflow

Records that are marked as deleted can be overwritten.

If there is no space in the correct block we say that a collision has occurred and there must be a method to store the record elsewhere.

One technique is to apply a rehashing algorithm based on the block that is full. This will, hopefully, give another block that is available. If this block is full the algorithm is reapplied using the new block. This is repeated until an empty block is found. The simplest rehashing algorithm is to store the record in the following block.

If no further information is provided, assume that overflow records are placed in the following block.

Another method is to use a separate overflow area (rather like the indexed sequential file). Each block has space for the address of an overflow block (Figure 40). When a record is placed in overflow the address of the overflow block used is stored in the correct block.

Key points from AS

- **Random file**
  Revise AS page 82

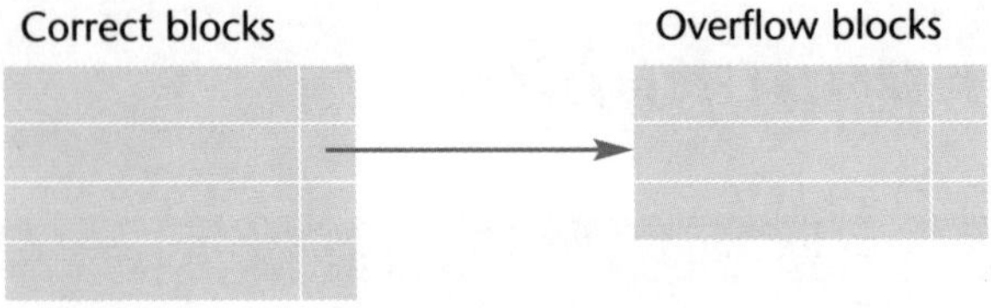

Figure 40

Progress check

In a stock control filing system for some 500 different items of stock, a hashing algorithm is applied to a seven-digit stock number to generate the disk address of the block which stores the data for each item of stock.

1 (a) State **one** problem that would arise if the seven-digit stock number were to be used directly as a disk address for this application. [1]

(b) Explain how the hashing algorithm overcomes this problem. [1]

2 With a disk block limited to holding the data for only one item of stock, how could the system deal with storing the data for two items of stock which generate the same disk address? [2]

AEB 1998

1 (a) The main point to make is that space will have to be reserved for every possible stock number as there will have to be as many blocks as there are possible stock numbers. This will cause the file to use up a large amount of space on the disk and there may not be enough space available.

(b) Hashing the stock numbers will produce a smaller range of addresses. This may allow the file to fit into the available space.

2 Insert the second record into an overflow area and mark the first record's block with a tag that indicates the overflow block that is used.

Another answer is to use an algorithm to find an alternative block within the range. If this is full the process is repeated until an empty block is found.

5.3 Relational databases

After studying this section you should be able to:

- *describe the structure of a database management system (DBMS)*
- *explain the term 'data definition language' (DDL)*
- *explain the term 'data manipulation language' (DML)*
- *perform entity-relationship modelling*
- *illustrate the use of Structured Query Language (SQL)*
- *use normalisation techniques*

LEARNING SUMMARY

Relational database features

AQA	M5
EDEXCEL	M4
OCR	M4
WJEC	CP5

When an application has its data stored in individual files we say that we are using a flat file system. Databases have many advantages over flat files as explained in the AS Guide. A relational database has a number of important features:

- tables – similar to files in a flat file system
- entities – similar to records in a flat file system
- attributes – similar to fields in a flat file system
- relationships – links between entities
- primary key – a unique identifier for an entity
- foreign key – a unique identifier for an entity in a different table
- secondary key – an alternative key for an entity.

Database management system

A database management system (DBMS) is a suite of programs that manipulate the database. The database will consist of a number of files that are stored on magnetic media but the user of the database will view the database as a single data store (Figure 41).

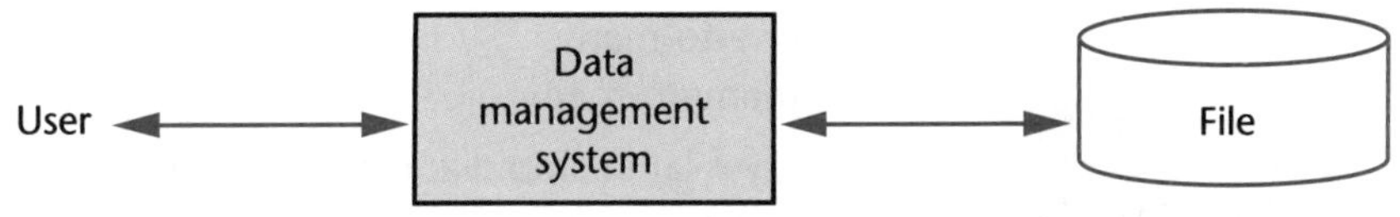

Figure 41

There are three main views of a database, known as the 'three-level architecture of a database management system'. Each view is known as a schema.

- The external schema will be the user's view of the database. Each user may well have a different external schema as they may be interested in different items of data.
- The conceptual schema is the overall view of the entire database.
- The internal or storage schema is concerned with the physical storage of the data. It will describe the files and storage media used to store the data.

The database management system will:

- create the database
- add and remove data from the database
- allow the user to query the database
- maintain the security and integrity of the database.

Key points from AS
- **Databases**
  Revise AS pages 85–86

The database management system will maintain a data dictionary that will record information about the data stored. Information to be stored in the data dictionary includes:

- name of each data item
- description of each data item
- type of data stored (e.g. character, integer, etc.)
- amount of storage required (e.g. number of characters)
- restrictions on data items (e.g. only characters in the range A to Z)
- relationships between items in the database
- which programs access the data items
- users access rights (i.e. who can access the data and whether they can update it).

A person known as a database administrator (DBA) will manage the database. This person's responsibilities include:

- designing the database
- maintaining the data dictionary
- implementing access rights to users
- monitoring the performance and updating the internal schema as appropriate
- providing training to the users
- keeping users informed of changes in the database that might affect them.

The database administrator will use a data definition language (DDL) to specify the database and a data manipulation language (DML) to manipulate the data. An example of a DML is the Structured Query Language (SQL) that is described later in this chapter.

> The database management system acts as the interface between the users and the database.
>
> KEY POINT

Relationships

A relational database consists of entities that may be related to other entities. A relationship will normally have a name and a degree. The degree may be one of:

- one-to-one
- one-to-many
- many-to-many.

There are several conventions but the generally accepted one for 'A' Level is the 'crow's foot' as shown.

Entity relationship diagrams are useful in illustrating the relationships in a database. The generally accepted standard is shown in Figure 42.

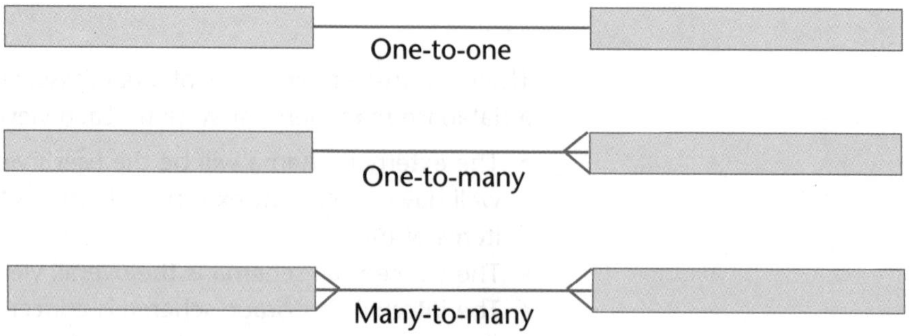

Figure 42

So a relationship between a teacher and a class of students might be called teaches and would be drawn as:

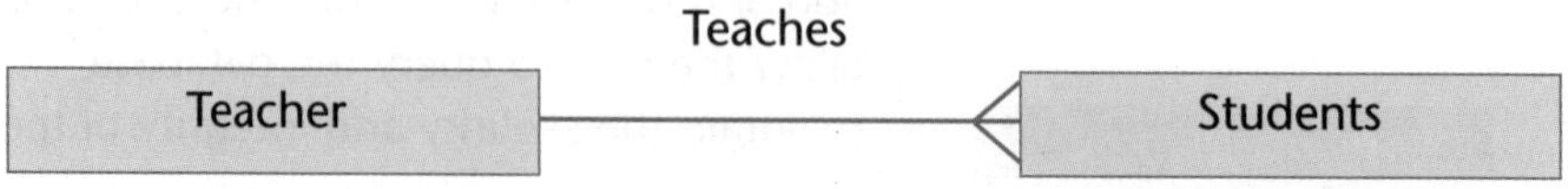

This is a one-to-many relationship as a single teacher has many students.

SQL is a comprehensive language but you will only be examined on a subset. You should ensure that you understand all the examples in this book.

Structured Query Language

Structured Query Language (SQL) is widely used to retrieve data from a relational database. For demonstration purposes let us consider the table in Figure 43 (named STUDENTS) that contains details of students attending a university.

STUDENTS Table

Surname	Forenames	Year	Subject
Evans	Gareth	1	English
King	Bridget	1	Mathematics
Harris	Linda	2	Computing
Turner	Teresa	2	Physics
Wong	Kevin	2	Philosophy
Brown	Kevin	2	Mathematics
Clark	James Robert	3	Computing
Livingstone	Henrietta	3	French
Pinter	Norman	3	Physics

Figure 43

The basic retrieval statement is SELECT and we can consider it to have the following format:

```
SELECT field_name {,field_name}*
FROM table_name {,table_name}
[WHERE search_condition]
[ORDER BY attribute_name {,attribute_name}]
;
```

- * is a special name which means select all fields
- {   } implies optionally one or more entries
- [   ] implies an optional entry.

FROM

The FROM clause specifies the table(s) to be used. An example is:

```
SELECT Surname, Forenames, Year, Subject FROM STUDENTS;
```

This would produce the complete STUDENTS table. Alternatively:

```
SELECT * FROM STUDENTS;
```

would produce the same result.

WHERE

One of the most useful features of the SQL query is that it allows you to selectively retrieve only those rows that interest you. In a large database, with thousands of rows in each table, you may only be interested in a handful of records at any time. The WHERE clause of the SELECT statement lets you specify a logical expression that can be either true or false. To select the physics students you could enter:

```
SELECT * FROM STUDENTS
WHERE Subject = 'Physics';
```

IN

What if you needed to check for certain values only? Values do not always fit into a neat range; the IN operator allows you to check whether values are in a set of allowed values. In the STUDENTS table, if we wanted to look at the rows of the mathematics and the computing subjects, we could use a query with IN:

```
SELECT * FROM STUDENTS
WHERE Subject IN ('Mathematics','Computing');
```

ORDER BY

The ORDER BY clause allows you to impose an order on the query results. You can use ORDER BY with one or more column names to specify the ordering of the query results. For example, to list students' records in alphabetical order by surname:

```
SELECT * FROM STUDENTS ORDER BY Surname;
```

> The SELECT statement allows the creation of a table of data from the tables of a relational database.
>
> KEY POINT

Normalisation

An attribute is often referred to as a field. The two terms are interchangeable.

A relation is unnormalised if it contains attributes that are repeated within a single entity. The table of SALES in Figure 44 illustrates this.

SALES Table

Customer_Id	Location	Distance	Item_No	Quantity
28374	Cambridge	15	2653	4
			5488	2
			9482	1
24933	Luton	10	3845	1
			4911	5
31102	Luton	10	9482	2
28330	Cambridge	15	2653	1
			3845	1
21126	Birmingham	20	4911	4

Figure 44

- Customer_Id is the identifier for a customer
- Location is the location of the customer
- Distance is the number of miles to the location
- Item_No is the identifier for an item
- Quantity is the number sold.

There would be other attributes such as Item Description but these have been left off for clarity.

First normal form (1NF)

1NF implies no repeating groups.

A table is said to be in first normal form if it contains no repeating attributes or groups of attributes. Item_No and Quantity are repeated in Figure 44. In 1NF, the table becomes that shown in Figure 45.

SALES Table

Customer_Id	Location	Distance	Item_No	Quantity
28374	Cambridge	15	2653	4
28374	Cambridge	15	5488	2
28374	Cambridge	15	9482	1
24933	Luton	10	3845	1
24933	Luton	10	4911	5
31102	Luton	10	9482	2
28330	Cambridge	15	2653	1
28330	Cambridge	15	3845	1
21126	Birmingham	20	4911	4

Figure 45

2NF implies that all attributes (fields) are dependent on the whole of the key.

Second normal form (2NF)

A table is in second normal form if it is in first normal form and no column that is not part of the primary key is dependent on only a portion of the primary key. The above table in 1NF can be described as follows:

SALES(Customer_Id, Item_No, Location, Distance, Quantity)

The primary key will be Customer_Id and Item_No. Location and Distance are not dependent on Item_No so they should be removed to another table.

SALES Table

Customer_Id	Item_No	Quantity
28374	2653	4
28374	5488	2
28374	9482	1
24933	3845	1
24933	4911	5
31102	9482	2
28330	2653	1
28330	3845	1
21126	4911	4

CUSTOMERS Table

Customer_Id	Location	Distance
28374	Cambridge	15
24933	Luton	10
31102	Luton	10
28330	Cambridge	15
21126	Birmingham	20

Figure 46

This gives us two tables in 2NF as follows:

- SALES(Customer_Id, Item_No, Quantity)
- CUSTOMERS(Customer_Id, Location, Distance).

These are shown in Figure 46.

3NF implies that no attributes (fields) are dependent on non-key attributes (fields).

Third normal form (3NF)

A table in third normal form contains no non-key dependencies. This implies that each attribute depends on the key and nothing else. In the example above, the Distance depends on the Location attribute and not on the key Customer_Id. To obtain 3NF we must create another table (Figure 47).

SALES Table

Customer_Id	Item_No	Quantity
28374	2653	4
28374	5488	2
28374	9482	1
24933	3845	1
24933	4911	5
31102	9482	2
28330	2653	1
28330	3845	1
21126	4911	4

CUSTOMERS Table

Customer_Id	Location	
28374	Cambridge	
24933	Luton	
31102	Luton	
28330	Cambridge	
21126	Birmingham	

TOWNS Table

Location	Distance	
Cambridge	15	
Luton	10	
Birmingham	20	

Figure 47

We now have three tables:

- SALES(Customer_Id, Item_No, Quantity)
- CUSTOMERS(Customer_Id, Location)
- TOWNS(Location, Distance).

> Third normal form means that *data items are dependent on the key only* and that *data items are dependent on all of the key.*
>
> KEY POINT

Progress check

The owner of a flower shop uses a relational database to store information about orders placed by customers, and the types of flower in stock.

1 One entity is defined as CUSTOMERS. List four attributes which you identify as belonging to this entity. [4]

2 Another entity is identified as the orders placed by customers (ORDERS). Explain the relationship between the entities CUSTOMERS and ORDERS [2]

3 A third entity is flowers, defined as the types of flower in stock. Draw an entity relationship diagram for the three entities in this database. [3]

4 Design a table in third normal form, called CUST, to hold the details of customers and explain why it is in third normal form. [2]

5 When a customer orders flowers, an order form has to be completed. The order form is shown below.

CUSTOMER ORDER

Order Number: **Date:** / /

Customer Number:

QUANTITY	FLOWER ID

(a) Create a table, called ORDER, which contains all the attributes shown on the order form. Explain why it is not normalised.

(b) Starting with the ORDER table, create a set of tables in third normal form.

(c) Explain how the tables can be used to create a list of customers who bought roses on 23/12/99. [7]

OCR 2509 Specimen

answers overleaf

Progress check (continued)

1 Any **four** from the following five options:
Forename, Surname
Address1, Address2, County
Postcode
Date of last order
Credit limit

2 One-to-many as each order is placed by one customer, but each customer may be responsible for more than one order.

3

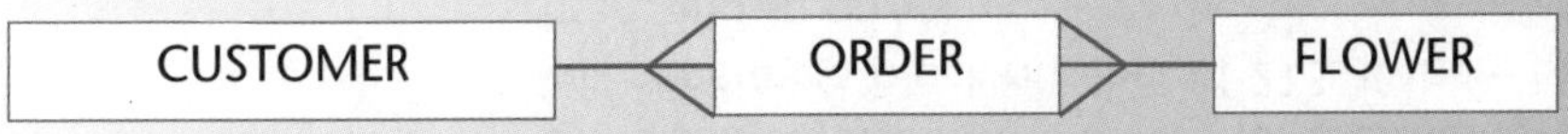

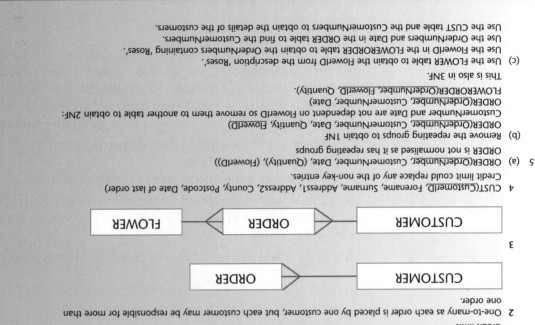

4 CUST(<u>CustomerID</u>, Forename, Surname, Address1, Address2, County, Postcode, Date of last order)
Credit limit could replace any of the non-key entries.

5 (a) ORDER(<u>OrderNumber</u>, CustomerNumber, Date, (Quantity), (FlowerID))
ORDER is not normalised as it has repeating groups

(b) Remove the repeating groups to obtain 1NF
ORDER(<u>OrderNumber</u>, CustomerNumber, Date, Quantity, <u>FlowerID</u>)
CustomerNumber and Date are not dependent on FlowerID so remove them to another table to obtain 2NF:
ORDER(<u>OrderNumber</u>, CustomerNumber, Date)
FLOWERORDER(<u>OrderNumber, FlowerID</u>, Quantity).
This is also in 3NF.

(c) Use the FLOWER table to obtain the FlowerID from the description 'Roses'.
Use the FlowerID in the FLOWERORDER table to obtain the OrderNumbers containing 'Roses'.
Use the OrderNumbers and Date in the ORDER table to find the CustomerNumbers.
Use the CUST table and the CustomerNumbers to obtain the details of the customers.

Sample questions and model answers

1

A video shop gives each of its members a small card that contains that person's membership number. The membership number is used to access the member's details that are held in a randomly organised file. The file is stored in 500 numbered blocks, each capable of holding two members' records. The following hashing algorithm produces the block number for a particular member's record.

1 Take the last three digits of the membership number.
2 Divide this number by two.
3 Block number is the integer part of the result of this division.

Using this algorithm the record for the member with membership number 1427 will generate a block number of 213. If there is a collision then the next block is tried, and so on.

(a) In the context of a randomly organised file, what is meant by a collision? [1]

(a) A collision occurs when a record is given a location by a hashing algorithm and that location is already full.

(b) Explain the steps involved in finding a record in a randomly organised file. [4]

(b) Hash the key field and search the specified location. If the record is not there, move to the first overflow block (possibly the next block in the file). Continue looking in overflow blocks until a gap is found. If a gap is found without obtaining the record, the record is not in the file.

(c) Six new members join the video club and are allocated the following membership numbers by a separate routine.

0462 1465 3464 1463 1464 4462

Given that the membership numbers are allocated in the order indicated above, into which block will each of their respective records be written? You can assume the relevant blocks are initially empty. [3]

(c) 0462 is stored in block 231
1465 is stored in block 232
3464 is stored in block 232
1463 is stored in block 231
1464 is stored in block 233

1464 should be stored in 232 but it is full.

4462 is stored in block 233

4462 should be stored in 231 but it is full and 232 is also full.

(d) If the member 1465 leaves the club, how would that person's record be discontinued without reorganising the file? [2]

(d) The record will be marked as deleted but the record will be left in position to allow future searching for records like 1464 and 4462.

If it was removed a gap would appear and searches for records like 1464 would fail.

(e) Explain the steps involved in adding a new record to the file. Include in your answer how collisions would be handled. [4]

Sample questions and model answers (continued)

Often the best way to explain an algorithm is to use pseudocode.

(e) Apply the hashing algorithm to the record key to obtain a block number.
While the record is not stored
    If there is a deleted record in that block overwrite it.
    else if there is a space add the record.
    If it is not possible to use this block look in the following block.
endWhile

NEAB 2000, CP05

2

A club, AQA Wanderers, wishes to computerise the records of matches played by its first team so that it can generate statistics on its players. The data requirements are defined below.

In a season, the club's first team plays against all opposition clubs' first teams from the same division of the league twice, once at home and once away from home. The date of each match, the start time, opposition team's name, whether home or away, goals for and goals against are recorded. Each AQA Wanderers' player has a player identification number and their surname, forenames, date of birth, contact telephone number are recorded.

For each match, fourteen players from a pool of twenty are selected as match players including three substitutes. The player identification numbers of the selected players are to be recorded for each match together with the identification number sewn on the shirt worn (range one to fourteen) so that a player's first-team appearances may be analysed. The goal scorers of AQA Wanderers, if any, in each match must also be recorded together with the number of goals scored by each against the opposition. Players one to eleven start the match but may be substituted by players twelve to fourteen during the match. For any substitution of an AQA Wanderers' player by another during a match the player identification numbers of both are to be recorded.

Five entities for AQA Wanderers are:

Player, MatchPlayer, Match, GoalScorer, Substitution

(a) Using a copy of the partially complete entity relationship diagram shown below as an aid show the degree of five more relationships which exist between the given entities.

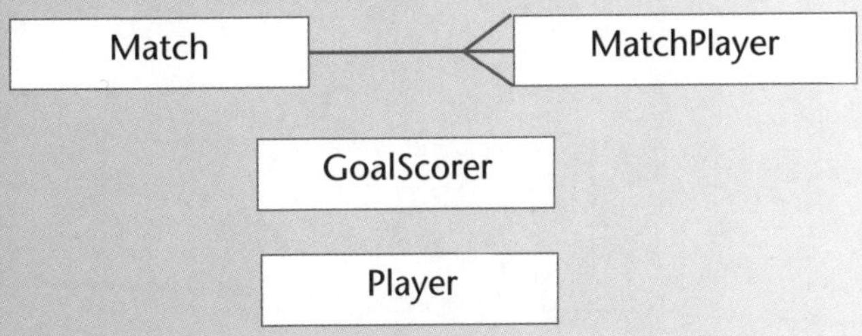

[5]

(a)

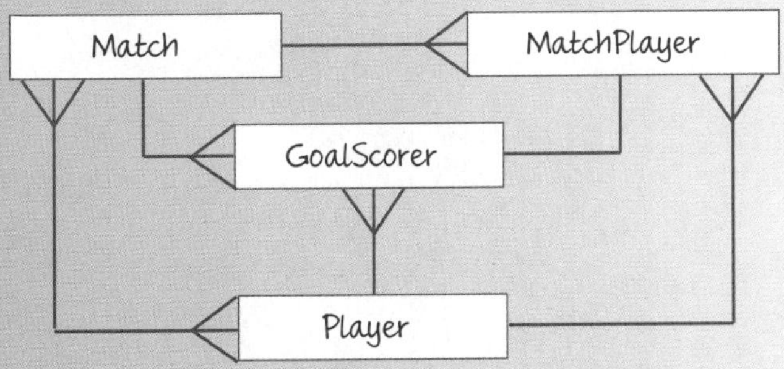

Sample questions and model answers (continued)

(b) A relational database is to be used to record the data for one season so that statistics on individual players can be produced at the end of the season. Using the following format:

TableName(<u>PrimaryKey</u>, Non-KeyAttribute1, NonKeyAttribute2, etc).

describe tables, stating all attributes, for the following entities, underlining the primary key in each case.

(i) Player [2]

(b) i) Player(<u>PlayerIdNo</u>, PlayerSurname, PlayerForenames, DOB, ContactTelNo)

(ii) Match [2]

Alternatively Match(<u>MatchDate</u>, OppositionTeamName, HomeAway, StartTime, GoalsFor, GoalsAgainst) as there should be only one match on one date.

(ii) Match(<u>OppositionTeamName, HomeAway</u>, MatchDate, StartTime, GoalsFor, GoalsAgainst)

(iii) GoalScorer [4]

Alternatively GoalScorer(<u>MatchDate, ShirtIdNo</u>, NoOfGoals).

(iii) GoalScorer(<u>MatchDate, PlayerIdNo</u>, NoOfGoals)

(iv) MatchPlayer [3]

Alternatively MatchPlayer(<u>MatchDate, ShirtIdNo</u>, PlayerIdNo).

(iv) MatchPlayer(<u>MatchDate, PlayerIdNo</u>, ShirtIdNo)

(v) Substitution [4]

Alternatively Substitution(<u>MatchDate, OnPlayerIdNo</u>, OffPlayerIdNo). You could also use ShirtIdNo instead of PlayerIdNo.

(v) Substitution(<u>MatchDate, OffPlayerIdNo</u>, OnPlayerIdNo)

AEB 1999, Paper 3

Practice examination questions

1 The data requirements for a league of cross-country running clubs are defined as follows.

The league consists of a number of participating clubs whose runners race each other in a series of races held throughout the season. The league secretary is responsible for recording data about clubs, races, race entries, race results and club league points.

Each race has a race identification number, date, start time, distance covered and venue recorded. Runners from different clubs compete in each race. Each club has its name (unique) and the name, address and telephone number of its results secretary recorded. On receipt of a race entry form from a club, the league secretary assigns each listed runner a competitor identification number in the range one to one hundred and their name and club name are recorded. This competitor identification number applies to that particular race only. A competitor's race time and position are recorded after each race. The points a club scores for each race are computed from the positions of its runners and recorded.

(a) Four entities for the league are Club, Race, ClubRacePoints and RaceCompetitor.

Draw an entity-relationship diagram which shows **four** relationships involving the entities Club, Race, ClubRacePoints and RaceCompetitor that can be inferred from the given data requirements. [4]

(b) A relational database is to be used. Using the following format

TableName(<u>Attribute1</u>, Attribute2, Attribute3, etc.)

describe tables, stating all attributes, for the following entities underlining the primary key in each case. **These are the only tables that are used.**

(i) Race [2]
(ii) Club [2]
(iii) RaceCompetitor [4]
(iv) ClubRacePoints [3]

(c) It is required to print out in race position order the results for a given race. The results are to consist of the competitor's name, club name, race position and race time. Using a query language, show how the required data may be extracted from the relevant table(s) in (b). [5]

AEB 1998, Paper 3

2 A large company employing over 50 000 employees, stores details of its employees for payroll purposes in an indexed sequential file with a multilevel index.

What is meant by a multilevel indexed sequential file? [3]

NEAB 1999, CP05

3 Each student at *Cader Idris* College is allocated to (exactly) one personal tutor, who is a lecturer in the college. Each of the lecturers uses a staff room, which he or she shares with one or more other lecturers. Most staff rooms have a telephone extension, though no staff room has more than one.

The table below shows part of the data held for a few of the students and their personal tutors. These data are held in a database.

Practice examination questions (continued)

Student Number	Student Name	Tutor Number	Tutor Name	Tutor Room	Tutor Telephone
6137	Morton, Lynne	407	Harris, Dave	215	492
6153	Khan, Imran	410	Adams, Jessica	214	495
6189	Evans, Elwyn	407	Harris, Dave	215	492
6192	Ho, Carol	408	Jones, Christine	220	
6207	Vernon, Wayne	407	Harris, Dave	215	492
6208	Dodd, Debbie	414	Buckley, Ruth	215	492
6226	Evans, Elwyn	414	Buckley, Ruth	215	492
6228	Alton, Chris	407	Harris, Dave	215	492
6231	Mir, Razwana	425	Beaumont, Jim	214	495
...	...	...	...	...	...

(a) (i) State **four** other fields which it would be useful to store about each student. [2]

(ii) State **four** other fields which it would be useful to store about each lecturer. [2]

(b) All the students are able to access some of the above data via the college network. Describe **two** restrictions that will be needed. Why is a database system particularly well suited to adding security? [3]

(c) (i) Explain the term *third normal form.* [2]

(ii) Restructure these data into third normal form. [6]

WJEC Specimen CP5

4 A bookshop uses a relational database to store details of its stock on a computer system. Two entities associated with this database are book and publisher. The key field (identifier) for the publisher entity is the publisher's name and for the book entity is the ISBN (International Standard Book Number).

(a) What is meant by a relational database? [2]

(b) State **four** attributes in addition to the ISBN and title associated with a book. [4]

(c) Draw a diagram showing the relationship between the book entity and the publisher entity. [2]

(d) State another entity that could be related to either of these entities. State the relationship involved and the key field (identifier) for the entity. [3]

NEAB 1999, CP05

5 Computer systems which require online access to files often use an indexed sequential organisation. Using this method of organisation, when a record will not fit into its designated area it is placed in overflow.

(a) Explain how overflow is managed. [2]

(b) Describe how a record which exists, but might not be in its designated area, is found when the indexed sequential file has two levels of index. [4]

(c) Once overflow has happened on a particular file why is it necessary to re-organise the file at the earliest opportunity? [2]

NEAB 1998, CP05

Chapter 6

Programming languages

The following topics are covered in this chapter:

- *Types of programming language*
- *Compilers and interpreters*
- *Procedural programs*
- *Object-oriented programs*
- *Declarative programs*

6.1 Types of programming language

After studying this section you should be able to:

- *explain the use of imperative programs*
- *explain the use of declarative programs*
- *explain the use of functional programs*
- *explain the use of object-oriented programs*
- *describe the use of visual programming languages*
- *describe the use of special-purpose programming languages*
- *describe what is meant by a fourth generation language*

LEARNING SUMMARY

The wide variety of programming languages

AQA	M4
EDEXCEL	M4, M5
OCR	M4
WJEC	CP4

There are many types of programming language. This is because there are so many types of programming problems to be solved. In some cases a special programming language is developed for a particular problem, but most programs are written in general-purpose programming languages. These can be categorised as:

- imperative (procedural)
- declarative
- functional
- object-oriented.

You will need to be familiar with one procedural language in order to improve your programming skills.

Most programs are written in procedural languages. Examples of procedural languages are PASCAL, C, COBOL, ALGOL, FORTRAN. Declarative languages, such as PROLOG, were developed for artificial intelligence (AI) systems. Functional programs consist of a series of functions, examples that you may be familiar with are LISP and LOGO. Object-oriented programming languages allow the development of object-oriented programs that are dealt with later in this chapter.

Visual programs

Visual programming languages have been developed to implement programs using a WIMP (Windows, Icon, Mouse and Pointer) environment. They have special features to manipulate the WIMP environment allowing the control of buttons, edit boxes, scroll boxes, radio buttons, check boxes, etc. Visual programs are normally object-oriented and event driven, that is they are executed when some event happens, such as a mouse button's being pressed. Examples are DELPHI, Visual C++ and Visual BASIC.

Key points from AS

- **Generations of program language**
  Revise AS pages 103–104

Fourth generation programs

The languages described so far are mostly third generation programming languages (3GL). There are now a number of fourth generation programming languages (4GL) available. A fourth generation language allows the program to be developed by creating the desired output or input visually. The code is then generated automatically. In a third generation language all the code has to be typed into the computer by hand.

Special-purpose languages

A number of languages have been developed for specific problems.

- PROLOG was developed specifically to solve artificial intelligence problems.
- There are special languages for simulation such as Simula. Simulation has special requirements to deal with queues and changing the time and date under the control of the program.
- There are special authoring programs that allow the development of teaching materials.
- Another specialist area is the development of web pages. There are also special fourth generation languages that allow the development of web pages very quickly.

KEY POINT

The type of problem should determine the programming language that is chosen.

Progress check

Explain, giving an example **in each case**, when you would use:

1 a fourth Generation programming language

2 a declarative programming language

3 a specialist programming language.

1 A fourth generation language would be used to develop a visual application. An example would be a web page.

2 A declarative language would be used for an artificial intelligence application. An example might be a medical diagnosis system. [Any AI application would do.]

3 Simulation is an area where a specialist program might be used. An example might be to simulate the movements of ships in a port. [Again, any simulation would do.]

6.2 Compilers and interpreters

LEARNING SUMMARY

After studying this section you should be able to:

- *describe the difference between compilation and interpretation*
- *describe what happens during lexical analysis*
- *describe what happens during syntax analysis*
- *describe what happens during code generation*
- *explain how errors are handled*
- *explain the use of linkers and loaders*
- *use Backus–Naur Form (BNF)*
- *use syntax diagrams*

Program translation

EDEXCEL M4
OCR M4
WJEC CP4

A compiler may well generate the target program in some intermediate code (sometimes known as p-code) rather than machine code.

Compiler

A compiler takes a computer program that is written by the programmer (the source program) and translates it into machine code (the target program). This process comprises three main steps, as illustrated in Figure 48.

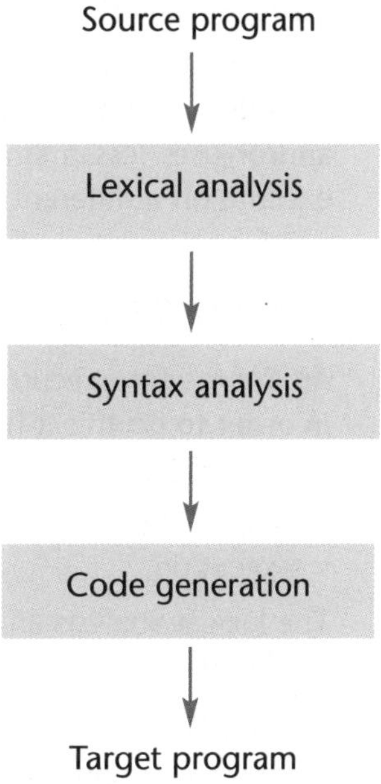

Figure 48

Lexical analysis

The main purpose of the lexical analyser is to convert the source program into a series of tokens that are passed on to the syntax analyser. The functions that the lexical analyser might perform include the following.

- Removing white space. White space is regarded as all the program code that is superfluous to the meaning of the programs and includes comments, spaces, tabs and new-line characters.
- Identify the individual words, operators, etc. (known as syntactic units) in the program.
- Create a symbol table. The symbol table will contain details of each symbol used in the program. A symbol might be a function name, a variable name, etc. The symbol table will be used by the later stages of the compiler. It will contain the symbol name plus information about the item, e.g. an integer, a procedure, etc.

Key points from AS

- **Translation programs**
  Revise AS page 60

- Some languages allow the use of include files. These are files of code that can be added to the program before compilation starts. The lexical analyser has to load these files.
- It keeps track of line numbers.
- It produces an output listing.
- Each reserved word, operator, etc. will be converted into a token to be passed to the syntax analyser.

Syntax analysis

The syntax analyser attempts to make sense of the program. There are two parts to this process:

- syntax analysis
- semantic analysis.

Syntax analysis discovers whether the program consists of valid statements as defined by the grammatical rules of the language, for example does a statement end with a semi-colon.

It is possible to have a statement that is syntactically correct but has no meaning. For example A := B; may be a correct PASCAL statement, but it is not possible to assign B to A if A is an integer variable and B is a character variable. Semantic analysis checks that the statements have some correct meaning.

Code generation

The result of code generation is a file of machine code, usually called an object file.

After syntax analysis the last stage is to generate the code. It may include an optimiser that takes the code and modifies it so that it executes more quickly and/or uses less memory. It is also possible to generate machine code that will execute on a different type of computer. This is known as cross-compilation.

Interpreter

An interpreter executes each line of code as it comes to it in the source program. In order to do this it has the following parts:

- lexical analysis
- syntax analysis
- execution.

The lexical analysis and the syntax analysis phases are similar to the compiler but the interpreter does not generate any code.

The advantages of an interpreter are:

- Interpreters are useful for program development when execution speed is not important. As the interpreter is in command of the execution process debugging features can be built in.
- It uses less memory than a compiler.

The advantages of a compiler are:

- A compiled program will always execute more quickly than one that is interpreted, as the interpreter has to understand every statement as it comes to it. This is most noticeable when executing a loop in a program. The interpreter will have to reinterpret each statement every time it goes through the loop.
- The target program (called the object program) can be stored on a disk and re-executed without being recompiled.
- Programs can be distributed in machine code form. This stops the user from modifying the program as they do not have access to the source code.

KEY POINT

Compilers and interpreters perform much the same task but are used in different circumstances.

Debugger

A debugger is often supplied with a compiler or interpreter. A debugger helps the programmer to find logical errors in the program. The compiler or interpreter will establish whether the program has broken any of the rules of the language but it cannot check whether the program is performing the correct task. A debugger can offer the following features:

- breakpoints – this stops the execution of the program at a predetermined point
- single step – to run the program one line at a time
- watches – to allow the programmer to inspect the contents of variables
- trace – provides a history of the statements executed immediately before the program failed
- store dump – provides details of the contents of the computer's memory.

Linking

Programs that make up a system are normally compiled separately and each compilation generates an object file. In order to build a system it is necessary to combine several object files and a linkage editor program performs this task. The result is a machine code file that is often known as an executable file and contains all the required object files linked together.

Libraries of prewritten routines are widely available for most programming languages.

It is also common practice to place regularly used programs in library files. A library is a file that contains a collection of object files. The linkage editor will manage these files and link them to other programs as necessary.

The loader is usually an integral part of the linkage editor.

In order to link object files, the files have to be copied into memory. It is also necessary to copy an executable file into memory before it can be executed. When program code is copied into memory we say that the code is loaded into memory. The program that performs this task is called a loader.

Backus–Naur Form

BNF is often known as a meta-language.

One method of specifying the grammatical rules (or syntax) of a language is Backus–Naur Form (BNF). BNF is a special type of language with a simple set of rules. The common symbols used are:

< >	used to enclose a syntactic category
::=	an operator meaning 'is defined by' or 'consists of'
|	is used to mean 'or'
{ }	zero or more repetitions of the contents

{ } are part of what is known as extended BNF, but you can use them.

BNF definitions are often recursive, for example a definition of an integer that contains one or more digits might be written:

<integer> ::= <digit> | <digit><integer>

<digit> ::= 0 | 1 | 2 | 3 | 4 | 5 | 6 | 7 | 8 | 9

Syntax diagrams

Another way of specifying the syntax of a language is to use syntax diagrams to define each valid item or statement. Consider an identifier in a typical program language. This starts with a letter and is followed by a number of letters or digits. Figure 49 illustrates how we might express this.

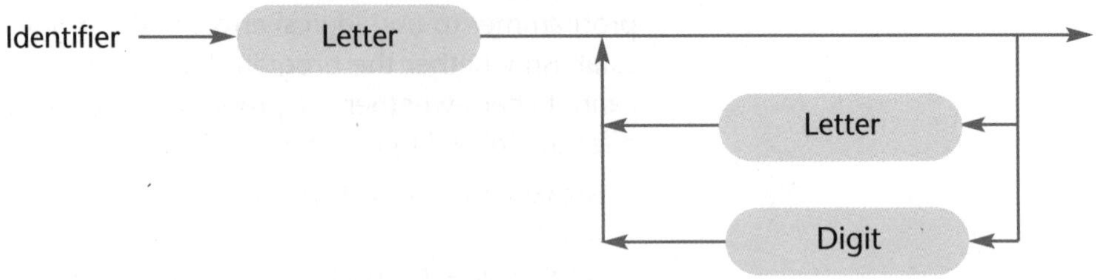

Figure 49

> **KEY POINT**
>
> BNF and syntax diagrams perform the same task in specifying syntax.

Progress check

An integer constant is defined as having an optional + or – sign followed by one or more digits.

1 Write a BNF specification of an integer constant.

2 Draw a syntax diagram of an integer constant.

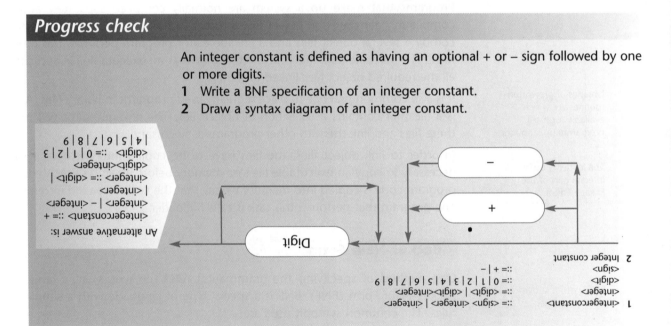

1 <integerconstant> ::= <sign> <integer> | <integer>
<integer> ::= <digit> | <digit><integer>
<digit> ::= 0 | 1 | 2 | 3 | 4 | 5 | 6 | 7 | 8 | 9
<sign> ::= + | –

2 Integer constant

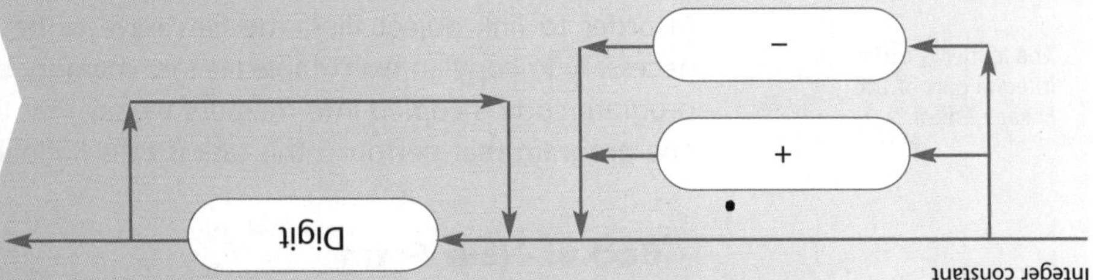

An alternative answer is:
<integerconstant> ::= + <integer> | – <integer> | <integer>
<integer> ::= <digit> | <digit><integer>
<digit> ::= 0 | 1 | 2 | 3 | 4 | 5 | 6 | 7 | 8 | 9

6.3 Procedural programs

After studying this section you should be able to:

- *explain how to develop structured programs*
- *describe the use of parameters*
- *explain how a stack is used to handle procedure calls*

LEARNING SUMMARY

Procedural programming techniques

AQA	M4
EDEXCEL	M4, M5
OCR	M4
WJEC	CP4

A common name for a function or procedure is a module.

Structured programming

Large programs need to be broken into smaller parts as it is difficult, if not impossible, to develop very large programs as a single piece of code. This is made possible by the use of procedures and functions. Each function or procedure can be written and tested individually. This leads to the possibility that a team of programmers can develop a large program in parts.

When a large program is broken down into smaller modules we call this top-down design. A method of describing a top-down design is a structure chart (Figure 50).

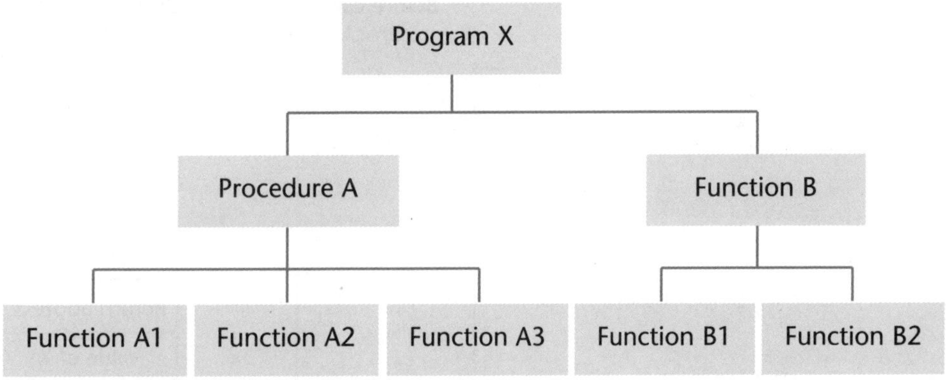

Figure 50

Pseudocode is a formal way of writing an algorithm using English statements. It should be very close to the final code.

The design of each function or procedure can be achieved by the use of pseudocode.

Parameters

The order and type of parameters that are passed to a function or procedure must match the parameters in the function or procedure header. There are two different methods of passing parameters:

- call by value
- call by reference.

A parameter that is passed by value will contain the value that is to be passed. Consider the following example.

```
ProcA(X)     /* a call to ProcA passing the parameter X by value */
Procedure ProcA(P1: integer)
Begin
          .
          .
End;
```

P1 will take the value in X. Any change to the value of P1 will not affect the value in X.

Key points from AS

- **Data types**
  Revise AS page 105
- **Programming statements**
  Revise AS pages 106–109

A parameter that is passed by reference will contain the address of the variable, not the value. This is achieved in Pascal by the keyword var. Other languages use other methods. Consider the following example.

```
ProcB(X)  /* a call to ProcB passing the parameter X by reference */
Procedure ProcB(var P1: integer)
Begin
        .
        .
        .
End;
```

P1 now points to the variable X. In this case changes to P1 will be reflected by a similar change to X.

Stack

The stack is used extensively for procedure (or function) calls. When a procedure is called the return address is stored on the stack. Parameters are also stored on the stack as are local variables of the procedure. Figure 51 shows what happens when Procedure A above (ProcA) is called.

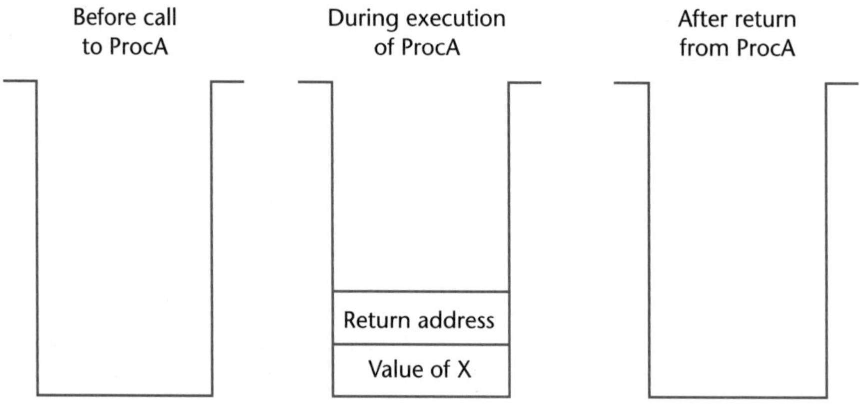

Figure 51

Progress check

The following piece of code forms part of a program

```
ProcH(A)   /* a procedure call to ProcH */
Procedure ProcH(P1: integer)
Begin
    ProcK;   /* a procedure call to ProcK */
```

Draw a diagram showing the contents of the stack when the program executes ProcK.

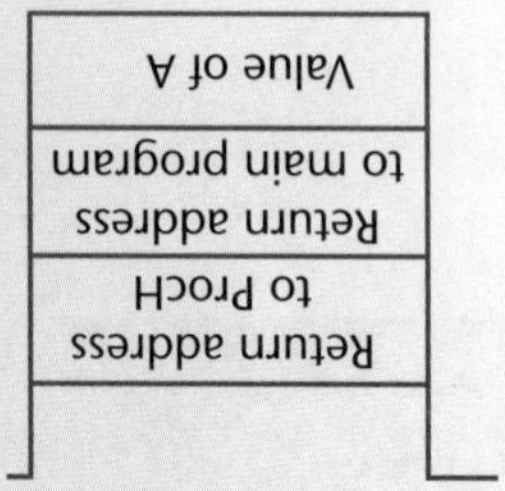

6.4 Object-oriented programs

After studying this section you should be able to:

LEARNING SUMMARY

- *describe what is meant by an object*
- *explain data encapsulation*
- *describe what is meant by a class*
- *explain what is meant by inheritance*
- *explain what is meant by polymorphism*

Features of object-oriented programs

AQA	M4
EDEXCEL	M4, M5
OCR	M4
WJEC	CP4

A computer system is normally a model of some real-life situation, and objects represent a closer imitation of real life.

Before object-oriented programming languages were available the data were stored in variables and programs performed the processing. The data and the processing were separate. An object-oriented program implements objects that contain both the data to represent those objects and the operations (usually called methods) that can be performed on them. This is a closer representation of real life. We say that the data and the operations are **encapsulated**.

An example might be a bank account. It has a certain state in that it will have an owner (the customer) and an amount. It will also have information about the customer and the credits and debits that have occurred. There will be a limited number of operations that you might wish to perform on a bank account. Examples are:

- credit an amount
- debit an amount
- provide the balance
- provide the customer's details.

Operations may be called methods or member functions in different object-oriented languages.

A class (short for classification) is a specification of an object. The bank account will be specified as a class (say BankAccount) that will contain details of both the data and the methods that are associated with a bank account. Any bank account objects can then be declared as of type BankAccount. A class is depicted as two rectangles with the state described in the upper box and the methods listed below (Figure 52).

<u>BankAccount</u> Account Number Customer Name Balance
Credit an amount Debit an amount Provide the balance Provide the customer's details

Figure 52

Inheritance

Once a class is written and tested other programmers can use it (known as reusability). Inheritance aids this process.

Suppose a bank decides to introduce a new account that pays interest. It will now require a new class with all the features of the BankAccount class plus an additional operation to add interest. Rather than rewriting (and retesting) the BankAccount class the programmer would use inheritance. Inheritance allows a new class to be derived from an existing class. A derived class will have all the features of the parent class plus any new features specified. In our example it will only be necessary to write the new operation.

Polymorphism

Another feature of object-oriented programming languages is polymorphism. This is a name given to the ability to have the same operation performing differently in different circumstances. This may mean that the same operation can operate on objects of different types. Operations are often implemented as functions or procedures and polymorphism allows an operation to perform differently depending on the parameters that are passed.

Progress check

The figure shows three classes called VEHICLE, CAR and LORRY.

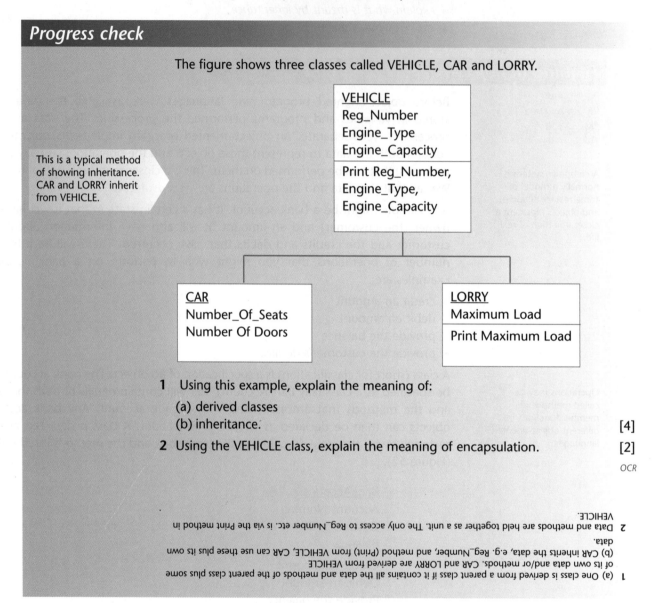

This is a typical method of showing inheritance. CAR and LORRY inherit from VEHICLE.

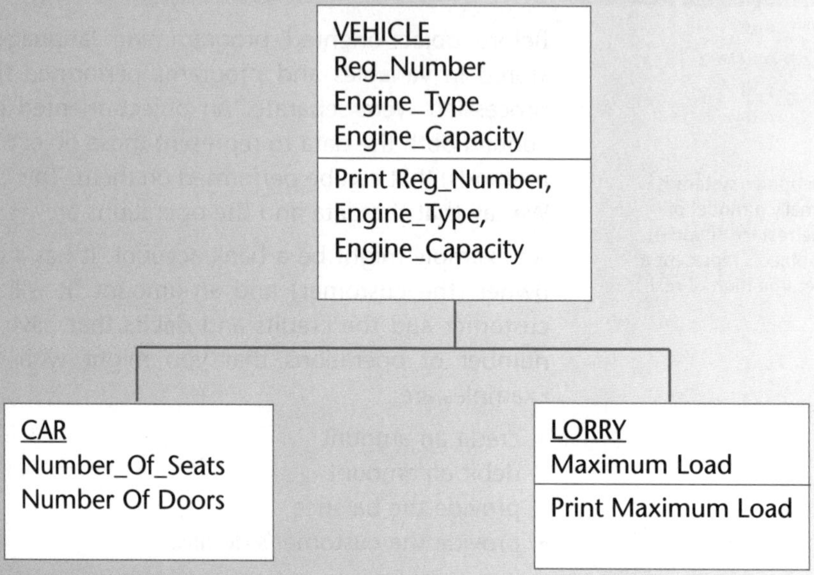

1 Using this example, explain the meaning of:

(a) derived classes

(b) inheritance. [4]

2 Using the VEHICLE class, explain the meaning of encapsulation. [2]

OCR

1 (a) One class is derived from a parent class if it contains all the data and methods of the parent class plus some of its own data and/or methods. CAR and LORRY are derived from VEHICLE

(b) CAR inherits the data, e.g. Reg_Number, and method (Print) from VEHICLE, CAR can use these plus its own data.

2 Data and methods are held together as a unit. The only access to Reg_Number etc. is via the Print method in VEHICLE.

6.5 Declarative programs

LEARNING SUMMARY

After studying this section you should be able to:

- *describe what is meant by a fact*
- *describe what is meant by a rule*
- *explain the satisfaction of goals*
- *describe backtracking*

Prolog

AQA	M4
EDEXCEL	M5
OCR	M4
WJEC	CP4

Prolog is an example of a different type of programming language known as declarative language. In Prolog the programmer does not write a series of instructions but derives a set of facts and rules. This set of facts and rules is stored in a Prolog database and the programmer asks Prolog a question in the form of a query. Prolog will attempt to solve the query by interrogating the database.

Prolog operates by attempting to satisfy a series of goals. For example a database may have the following facts and rules:

1 parent(jim,joan)
2 parent(mark,linda)
3 parent(sarah,joan)
4 parent(jim,kevin)
5 parent(sarah,kevin)
6 female(joan)
7 female(linda)
8 female(sarah)
9 male(mark)
10 male(kevin)
11 father(A,B) IF parent(A,B) AND male(A)
12 mother(A,B) IF parent(A,B) AND female(A)

Clauses 1 to 10 are facts. Clauses 11 and 12 are rules. A capital letter denotes a variable. A query can take the form: mother(sarah,joan)?

This becomes a goal and Prolog will attempt to satisfy this goal as follows.

- Prolog will use rule 15 by looking for parent(sarah,joan). This is known as a sub-goal.
- Having found this in fact 3, Prolog will attempt to satisfy the goal female(sarah). It finds this in fact 10 and will return Yes as a response.

Another query might be: mother(X,joan)

- Prolog will use rule 15 to attempt to satisfy this goal.
- The first sub-goal is parent(X,joan). Prolog will find parent(jim,joan).
- Prolog will now attempt to satisfy female(jim).
- At this point Prolog will fail to satisfy the goal. It will not give up, it will backtrack to the sub-goal parent(X,joan) and continue down the database. It will now find parent(sarah,joan).
- Prolog will now attempt to satisfy the sub-goal female(sarah).
- This is successful and Prolog will provide X is sarah.

Progress check

Write a rule to define the relation sister(X,Y).

sister(X,Y) IF father(A,X) AND father(A,Y)
AND mother(B,X) AND mother(B,Y).

Sample questions and model answers

1

(a) Analysts and programmers sometimes need to choose between programming languages.
For instance, a programmer might have to choose between an *imperative* and a *declarative* language.

(i) Explain what is meant by a an imperative language, and state an example of an application which could sensibly use an imperative language. [2]

(a) (i) Statements of an imperative language are usually actions/procedures to be carried out.

Almost any example will suffice where a number of actions are required, (e.g. payroll, stock control, games program).

(ii) Explain what is meant by a declarative language, and state an example of an application which could sensibly use a declarative language. [2]

(ii) Statements of a declarative language are usually facts and/or rules.

An example could be artificial intelligence, knowledge-based system, expert system.

(b) A programmer is required to write a program to simulate the arrival of trains at a busy station. He/she has the choice of a specialist simulation language or a general-purpose language.

Describe one advantage of each type of language. [2]

(b) A specialist simulation language will have special features of use in simulation, e.g. time/clock features, queues.

A general-purpose language will have a number of advantages. Any one of the following would do:

The language may be familiar so there is no need to learn a language specially.

No need to purchase extra software.

It will be able to interface with other parts of a system.

It may be easier to maintain in future (less specialist knowledge required).

(c) A certain programmer chooses to use an object-oriented approach, using a visual programming language. Explain the two terms object-oriented and visual programming languages and describe two advantages which their use might have over a more traditional approach. [4]

WJEC Specimen CP4

(c) An object-oriented language defines the data types and the allowable operations at the same time.

A visual programming language allows easy creation and manipulation of screen windows, buttons, etc.
Either of the following are advantages of object-oriented programs:
Combining data and processing is a more intuitive approach.
Tends to be more reliable/easier to maintain because of the separation into objects.
Either of the following are advantages of visual programming:
Promotes rapid application development.
Allows development of systems with reduced need for traditional programming.

Sample questions and model answers (continued)

2

(a) Explain why a compiled program will normally execute faster than an interpreted program. [2]

(a) Each time an interpreted program loops, translation is necessary whereas with a compiled program, this translation is done before execution starts.

(b) Most programming environments include some sort of debugging software.

(i) One example of debugging software is a *program trace*. Explain the term program trace. [1]

(b) (i) It allows step-by-step observation/operation of the program.

(ii) Give an example of an error which debugging software will not be able to find. [1]

(ii) A logical error, e.g. program includes line total := a − b instead of correct total := a + b

(c) Compilation of a high level language includes the following processes. Describe each of these processes:

(i) *lexical analysis*

(c) (i) Lexical analysis – any two from:
Breaks up the input stream into tokens.
Removes comments, unneeded spaces.
Checks all tokens are valid.
Generates error messages if appropriate.

You will not get marks for generating error messages in both (i) and (ii). You should always look for features that are distinct.

WJEC Specimen CP4

(ii) Syntax analysis.

(ii) Syntax analysis – any two from:
Determines whether the string of tokens fits the grammar of the language, using BNF or similar rules.
Generates dictionary or symbol table.
It generates error messages when it is unable to complete its task.

3

The following expresses family relationships using the declarative paradigm.

mary	childof	fred
mary	childof	anne
john	childof	fred
john	childof	anne
frank	childof	mary
edna	childof	john

X grandchildof Z if
X childof Y and
Y childof Z

(a) Show how instantiation is used to satisfy the goal

X childof fred [2]

If it is repeated, X is instantiated to John.

(a) X childof fred is compared to first line, fred matches so X is replaced, instantiated to mary and goal is satisfied

(b) Show how instantiation and backtracking are used to satisfy the goal
W grandchildof fred [4]

OCR 2509 Specimen

Sample questions and model answers (continued)

If it is repeated, edna will be found.

(b) W grandchildof fred becomes W childof Y and Y childof fred. As in (a), Y becomes mary and new goal is W childof mary and mary childof fred. W is instantiated to frank. There are no more matches so backtrack to Y childof fred and find the other match Y is John.

4

Use extended Backus–Naur Form (BNF) to define the syntax for the following:

(a) a single digit between 0 and 9 inclusive [1]

(a) <digit> ::= 0 | 1 | 2 | 3 | 4 | 5 | 6 | 7 | 8 | 9

(b) a signed integer with one or more digits [2]

(b) <sign> ::= + | − <signed integer> ::= <sign> <digit> {<digit>}

(c) a signed real number where there must always be at least one digit before and one digit after the decimal point. [3]

An alternative answer is: <signed real> ::= <sign> <digit> {<digit>} . <digit> {<digit>}

(c) <signed real> ::= <signed integer> . <digit> {<digit>}

NEAB 1998, CP04

Practice examination questions

1 (a) Briefly explain the difference between the use of a compiler and an interpreter in the translation of a high-level language program into executable form. [4]

(b) Suggest in what circumstances it would be appropriate to use:

(i) a compiler rather than an interpreter; [2]

(ii) an interpreter rather than a compiler. [2]

(c) Explain how a stack can be used to control calls to procedures. [4]

OCR 2509 Specimen

2 Three types of program error are translation, linking and execution errors. Give **one** example of each. [3]

NEAB 1999, CP04

3 Draw a syntax diagram to show the rules for an identifier in a language where all identifiers must start with a letter and can contain only upper-case letters and digits. Upper-case letter and digit are already defined. [4]

NEAB 1999, CP04

4 A particular functional language has the following functions available:

p (a, b)	a function which returns the value of a * b
s (a, b)	a function which returns the value of a + b
e (a, b)	a function which returns the Boolean value true if a is equal to b otherwise it returns false
i (n , a, b)	a function that returns the value a if the Boolean value n is true else it returns the value b

(a) Given that the variable x contains the value 5 and the variable y contains the value 7, what value is returned to the variable answer, using the following:
answer := i(e(x,3),s(x,y),p(x,y))? [1]

(b) Using the functional language given above write down the functional equivalent of the following pseudocode statement.

```
if y = 7 then
    answer := 4 * x + y
else
    answer := 3 * x
endif
```

[4]

NEAB 1998, CP04

5 A simple logic programming language is used to represent, as a set of facts and rules, the syntax of sentences in a subset of English language. The set of facts and rules are shown below in clauses labelled 1 to 16.

1 determiner(a)
2 determiner(the)
3 adjective(big)
4 noun(monkey)
5 noun(peanut)
6 noun(cat)
7 verb(ate)
8 verb(chased)
9 adverb(quickly)
10 noun_phrase(X) IF noun(X)
11 noun_phrase(X,Y) IF determiner(X) AND noun(Y)

Practice examination questions *(continued)*

12 noun_phrase(X,Y,Z) IF determiner(X) AND adjective(Y) AND noun(Z)
13 verb_phrase(X) IF verb(X)
14 verb_phrase(X,Y) IF adverb(X) AND verb(Y)
15 sentence(A,B,C) IF noun_phrase(A) AND verb_phrase(B) AND noun_phrase(C)
16 sentence(A,B,C,D,E) IF noun_phrase(A,B) AND verb_phrase(C) AND noun_phrase(D,E)

In the set of facts and rules above, variables are single letters in upper-case, e.g. A and B.

Clause 3 has the meaning 'big is an adjective'
Clause 8 has the meaning 'chased is a verb'
Clause 11 has the meaning 'X followed by Y is a noun phrase if X is a determiner and Y is a noun'

(a) Explain the term syntax. [1]

(b) Using the given set of facts and rules (1–16 above), give one example of
 (i) a fact [1]
 (ii) a rule. [1]

(c) Using the given set of facts and rules (1–16 above), state whether or not the following sentences are valid, indicating which rules have been applied in the process.
 (i) the monkey ate the peanut [2]
 (ii) a peanut ate the monkey [2]

(d) The sentence 'the monkey chased the big cat quickly' is not a valid sentence according to the given set of facts and rules. Write a rule or rules that make this sentence valid. [5]

(e) In another application, the logic programming language is used to construct the syntax analyser phase of a compiler for a programming language.
 (i) Give **two** reasons why this is a simpler task than writing a syntax analyser for the whole of the English language. [2]
 (ii) An earlier phase of the compiler is the lexical analyser. State **four** functions carried out by this phase. [4]
 (iii) Explain why lexical and syntax analysis alone are insufficient to decide on the validity of a program statement. Illustrate your answer with at least one example. [2]

AEB 1998, Paper 3

Chapter 7

Algorithms

The following topics are covered in this chapter:

- *Pseudocode*
- *Recursion*
- *Linked lists*
- *Stacks*
- *Queues*
- *Binary trees*
- *Sorting and searching algorithms*

7.1 Pseudocode

After studying this section you should be able to:

- *describe algorithms using pseudocode*

LEARNING SUMMARY

Constructing an algorithm

AQA	M4
EDEXCEL	M5
OCR	M4
WJEC	CP4

An algorithm is a sequence of instructions to solve a given problem. There are many different ways of expressing algorithms but an excellent method is to use pseudocode. Pseudocode is a name given to a formal method of writing down the steps involved in an algorithm and is close to the final program code. It has all the constructs that you might expect in a program language. Typical pseudocode constructs include:

Some writers use upper case for the constructs and lower case for the rest of the algorithm but it is not a fixed rule.

- PROCEDURE ... ENDPROC
- FUNCTION ... ENDFUN
- IF ... THEN ... ELSE ... ENDIF
- WHILE ... DO ... ENDWHILE
- REPEAT ... UNTIL
- FOR ... TO ... ENDFOR
- CASE ... OF ... ENDCASE

Most pseudocode will use the above constructs but there are no fixed rules about pseudocode and you may see other approaches. The nice thing about pseudocode is that you can largely ignore syntax rules as long as the code makes sense. The line of Pascal code

```
X := 6;
```

can be written in pseudocode as:

```
X := 6
Set X to be 6
X ← 6
Put 6 in X
```

or any other statement that means the same. In the same way, we do not worry about declaring variables, and if you are not sure how to do something simply write in English what it is you hope to achieve.

The algorithms in this chapter will generally be expressed in pseudocode.

Key points from AS

- **Algorithms**
  Revise AS pages 110–112

7.2 Recursion

After studying this section you should be able to:

- *use recursive techniques*

LEARNING SUMMARY

Definition and application

AQA	M4
EDEXCEL	M5
OCR	M4
WJEC	CP4

You will not normally be asked to write recursive algorithms but you may be asked to understand them.

Recursion is a very powerful technique that can be used when programming an algorithm in which there is a variable number of iterations. Recursive routines have two important features:

- a recursive routine calls itself
- it must have a terminating condition.

As a recursive routine calls itself there must be a way of stopping it or it will continue to call itself for ever in a continuous loop.

An example is a procedure to produce a list of the square numbers. The procedure will be passed two parameters stating what the largest and smallest squares should be. This can be written non-recursively using a while loop as follows:

```
PROCEDURE Squares(Low, High)
        Count := Low
        WHILE Count <= High
            PRINT (Count * Count)
            Add 1 to Count
        ENDWHILE
ENDPROC
```

This could be written as a recursive procedure as follows:

```
PROCEDURE Squares(Low, High)
          IF Low <= High              /* Terminating condition */
              PRINT (Low * Low)
              Squares(Low+1,High)         /* recursive call */
          ENDIF
ENDPROC
```

Recursive routines have an if statement (**not** a while) to specify the terminating condition.

The recursive call asks that Squares be executed again with new parameters. Figure 53 sets out how you might trace a call to Squares(1,3).

	1st call		2nd call		3rd call		4th call		
Instruction	Low	High	Low	High	Low	High	Low	High	Output
Squares(Low,High)	1	3							
IF Low <= High									
PRINT(Low*Low)									1
Squares(Low+1,High)			2	3					
IF Low <= High									
PRINT(Low*Low)									4
Squares(Low+1,High)					3	3			
IF Low <= High									
PRINT(Low*Low)									9
Squares(Low+1,High)							4	3	
IF Low <= High									
ENDIF									
ENDPROC									
ENDIF									
ENDPROC									
ENDIF									
ENDPROC									
ENDIF									
ENDPROC									

Figure 53

Recursive calls are possible only if the system uses a stack to store the parameters and the return addresses.

You can see from the trace table that Squares is called four times. After Squares is completed it returns to the statement following the recursive call (which is the ENDIF in this case). A useful hint is that lines of code that occur before the recursive call will be executed in the order of the calls, lines of code after the recursive call will be executed in reverse order.

Progress check

A trace is not particularly difficult as long as you take care and don't rush. Be sure to put down every step, do not attempt to take short-cuts.

The following is a recursive algorithm:

```
PROCEDURE ProcA(Low,High)
    IF Low < High THEN
            ProcA(Low+1,High)
    ENDIF
    PRINT (Low * High)
ENDPROC
```

Trace the call ProcA(2,4).

answer overleaf

Progress check *(continued)*

Instruction	1st Call		2nd Call		3rd Call		
Instruction	Low	High	Low	High	Low	High	Output
ProcA(Low,High)	2	4					
IF Low < High							
ProcA(Low+1,High)			3	4			
IF Low < High							
ProcA(Low+1,High)					4	4	
IF Low < High							
PRINT(Low*High)							16
ENDIF							
ENDPROC							
ENDIF							
PRINT(Low*High)							12
ENDPROC							
ENDIF							
PRINT(Low*High)							8
ENDPROC							

7.3 Linked lists

After studying this section you should be able to:

- *explain the concept of a linked list*
- *describe methods of representing a linked list*
- *describe the algorithms used to manipulate a linked list*

LEARNING SUMMARY

Constructing and manipulating linked lists

AQA	M4
EDEXCEL	M5
OCR	M4
WJEC	CP4

Linked lists offer a dynamic data store, they are not fixed size like arrays.

A linked list will normally have a start pointer and nodes containing the data linked together:

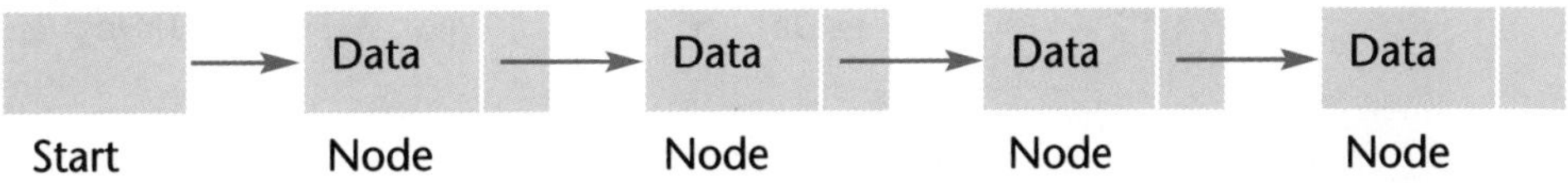

The final node in the list will have a pointer that contains a null value. The tricky algorithms involve removing and adding nodes to this list.

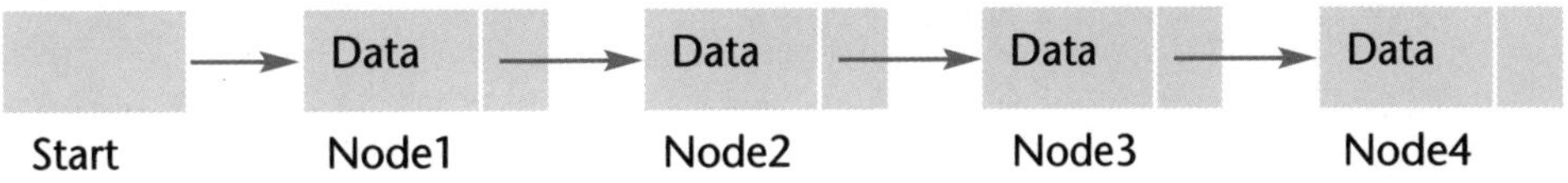

Let us assume that we wish to remove Node2 from the above. The first step is to change the pointer from Node1 to point at Node3:

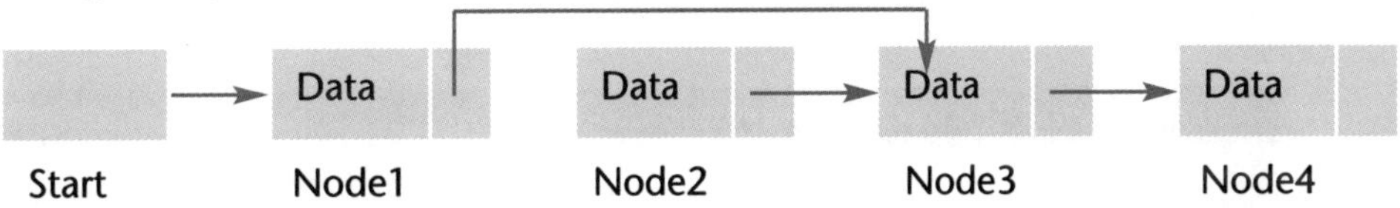

Node2 can now be disposed of:

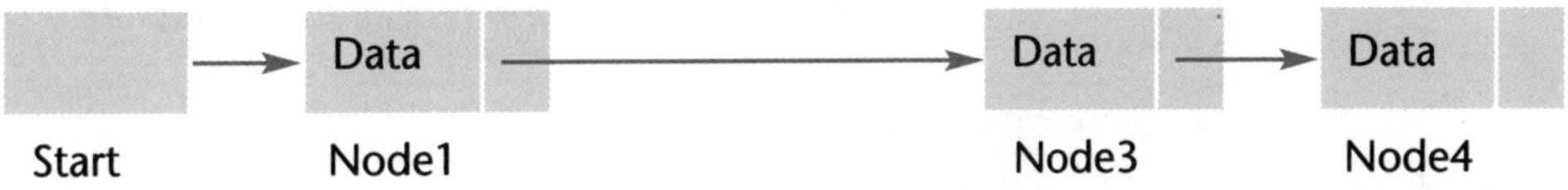

A language that supports dynamic data structures will have a Dispose operation.

Let us assume that we wish to add a new node between Node3 and Node4. The first step is to create a new node:

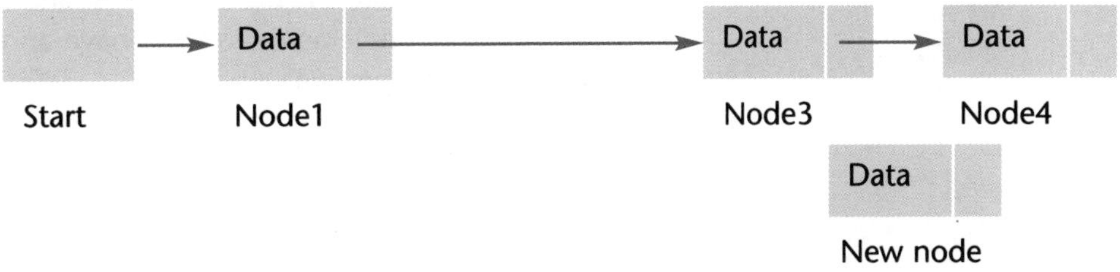

The pointer from Node3 must now be made to point to the new node and the new node must point to Node4:

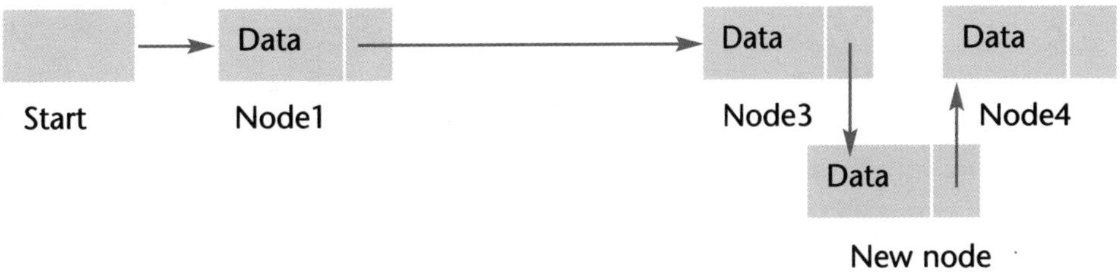

Progress check

A linked list consists of a variable START that points to the first node and a number of linked nodes. Each node has a variable DATA that contains a data item and a variable NEXT that is a pointer to the next node. The linked list has the following data items:

Harry Marion Sarah Bill Teresa

(a) Draw a diagram of the linked list.

(b) Explain how Sarah can be removed from the list.

(a)

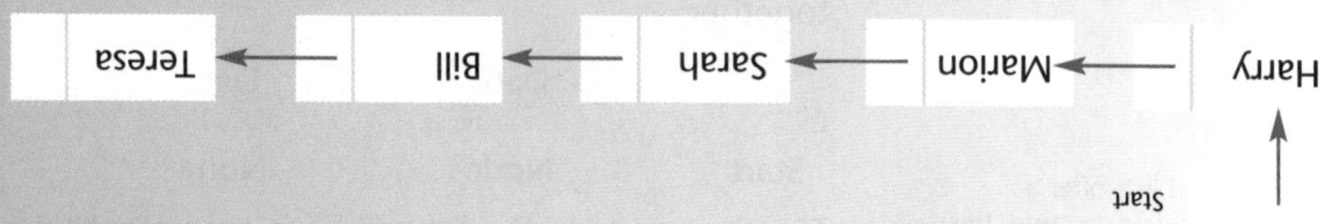

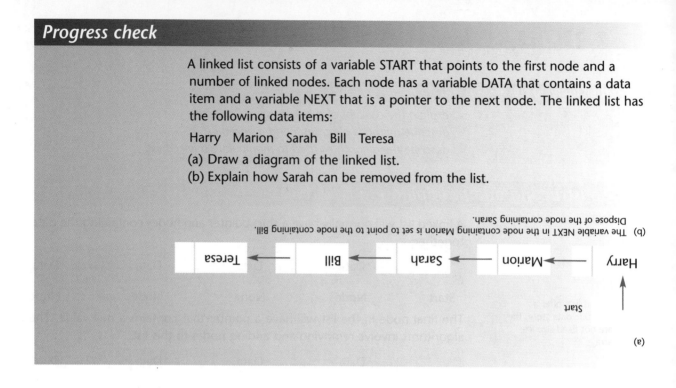

(b) The variable NEXT in the node containing Marion is set to point to the node containing Bill. Dispose of the node containing Sarah.

7.4 Stacks

LEARNING SUMMARY

After studying this section you should be able to:

- *explain the concept of a stack*
- *describe methods of representing a stack*
- *describe the algorithms used to manipulate a stack*

Implementing stacks

AQA	M4
EDEXCEL	M5
OCR	M4
WJEC	CP4

A stack can be implemented as a linked list or an array. In the case of a linked list, a new item is added to the front of the list and Pop takes an item from the front of the list. An array implementation will have an array plus a variable to record the top of the stack (Figure 54).

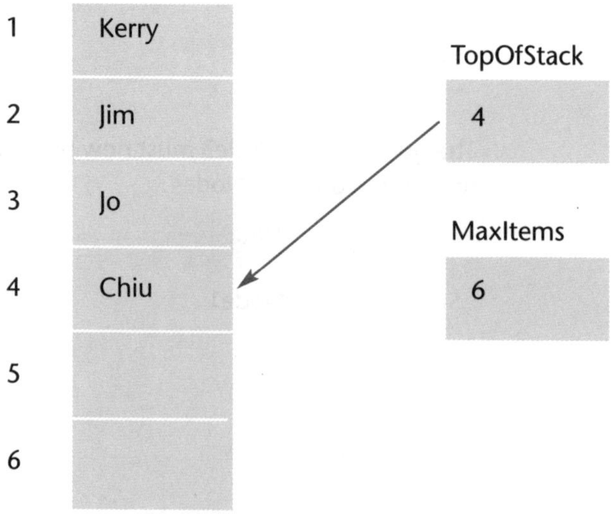

Figure 54

There will be another variable to indicate the maximum number of items that can be stored in the stack (say MaxItems). The procedure to add an item to the stack (Push) might be:

```
PROCEDURE Push(inItem)
        IF TopOfStack = MaxItems
            THEN Output "Stack is Full"
        ELSE
            Add 1 to TopOfStack
            Stack[TopOfStack] := inItem
        ENDIF
ENDPROC
```

To remove an item (Pop):

```
PROCEDURE Pop(outItem)/* outItem must be passed by reference */
        IF TopOfStack = 0
            THEN Output "Stack is empty"
        ELSE
            outItem := Stack[TopOfStack]
            Subtract 1 from TopOfStack
        ENDIF
ENDPROC
```

Progress check

Using the array implementation described above, write a pseudocode algorithm to print the top item from the stack.

Do not worry overmuch about the style of your pseudocode. The examiner will be marking the logic of your algorithm, not the style.

```
PROCEDURE Top
IF TopOfStack = 0
THEN PRINT "Stack is empty"
ELSE
PRINT stack[TopOfStack]
ENDIF
ENDPROC
```

7.5 Queues

LEARNING SUMMARY

After studying this section you should be able to:

- *explain the concept of a queue*
- *describe methods of representing a queue*
- *describe the algorithms used to manipulate a queue*

Implementing queues

AQA M4
EDEXCEL M4
OCR M4
WJEC CP4

A queue is a FIFO structure in that it adds items to the back of the queue and takes items from the front. If this is implemented as a linked list the linked list operations will take care of this, but an array implementation needs a special approach. The items can be stored in an array together with two variables:

- Front – to indicate the item at the front of the queue
- Rear – to indicate the item at the back of the queue.

It can also be useful to have two additional variables:

- NoInQ – number of items in the queue
- MaxSize – the maximum size of the queue.

Let us suppose we have a queue containing Terry, Lim, Mark and Tamsin (Figure 55).

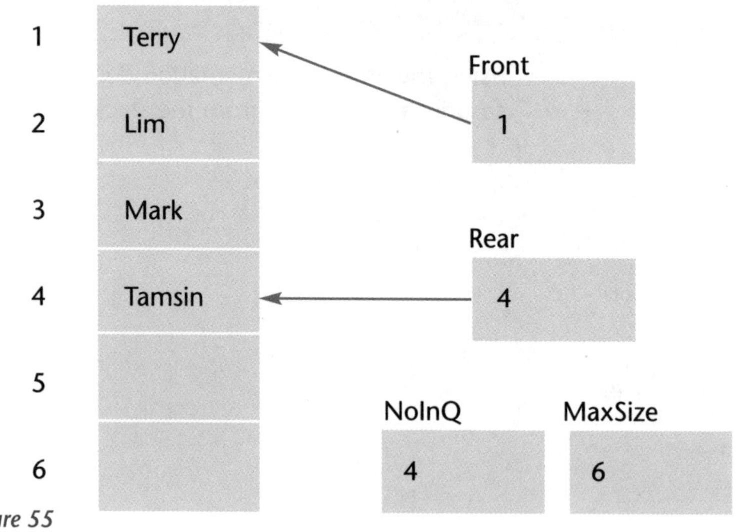

Figure 55

As items are added and removed the items move down the array until they reach the end. Let us assume that Terry, Lim and Mark are removed and Ursula and Norma are added. Figure 56 shows the new queue.

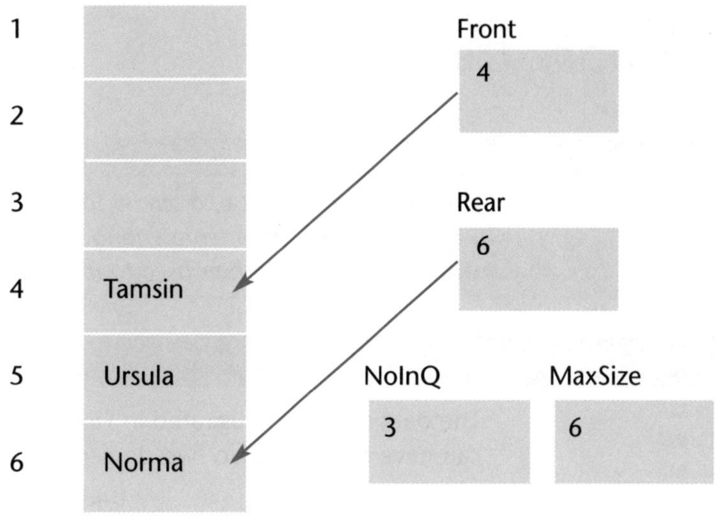

Figure 56

The next item must be added in position 1. We say that we are implementing a circular array (see section 3.3 in Chapter 3). A procedure to add an element to such a queue might be:

```
PROCEDURE ADD(inItem)
        IF NoInQ = MaxSize
            THEN output "Queue Full"
        ELSE
            IF Rear = 6         }
                THEN Rear := 1  }
            ELSE                }   A better solution is
                Add 1 to Rear   }   Rear := (Rear Mod 6) + 1
            ENDIF               }
            Queue[Rear] := inItem
            Add 1 to NoInQ
        ENDIF
ENDPROC
```

In this case an even better solution would use MaxSize in place of the integer 6.

Progress check

Write a pseudocode procedure to remove an item from the queue. It is not necessary to return the item, simply to remove it.

```
PROCEDURE Remove
IF NoInQ = 0 THEN PRINT "Queue Empty"
ELSE
    IF Front = 6 THEN Front := 1
    ELSE   Add 1 to Front
    ENDIF
    Subtract 1 from NoInQ
ENDIF
ENDPROC
```

or

```
PROCEDURE Remove
    IF NoInQ = 0
    THEN PRINT "Queue Empty"
    ELSE
        Front := (Front Mod 6) + 1
        Subtract 1 from NoInQ
    ENDIF
ENDPROC
```

7.6 Binary trees

After studying this section you should be able to:

- explain the concept of a binary tree
- describe methods of representing a binary tree
- describe the algorithms used to manipulate a binary tree

LEARNING SUMMARY

Structure and use of binary trees

AQA	M4
EDEXCEL	M5
OCR	M4
WJEC	CP4

There are many types of tree but you should only meet binary trees on this course.

The data structure illustrated in Figure 57 is a binary tree. In a binary tree, a node can have no more than two descendants.

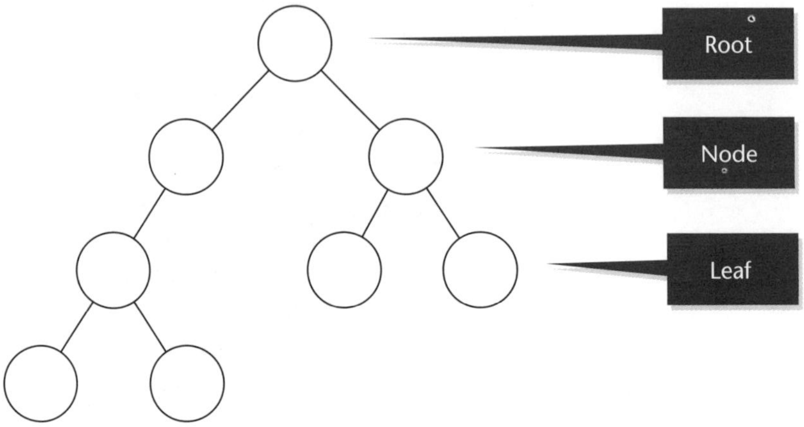

Figure 57

The descendants are known as the left child, or left descendant, and right child, or right descendant (Figure 58).

A binary tree node is like a linked list node but with two pointers, LeftChild and RightChild.

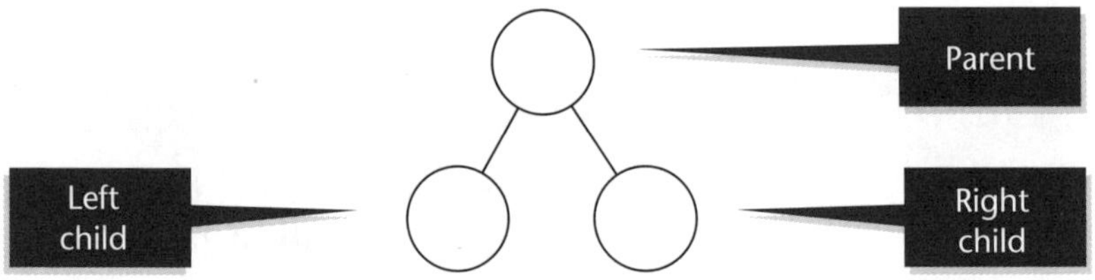

Figure 58

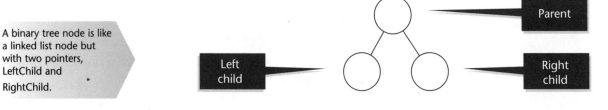

Binary trees can be used in many ways. One use is to hold an ordered set of data. In an ordered binary tree all items to the left of the root will have a smaller key than those on the right of the root. This applies equally to all the sub-trees. An example is:

Tree algorithms are invariably recursive.

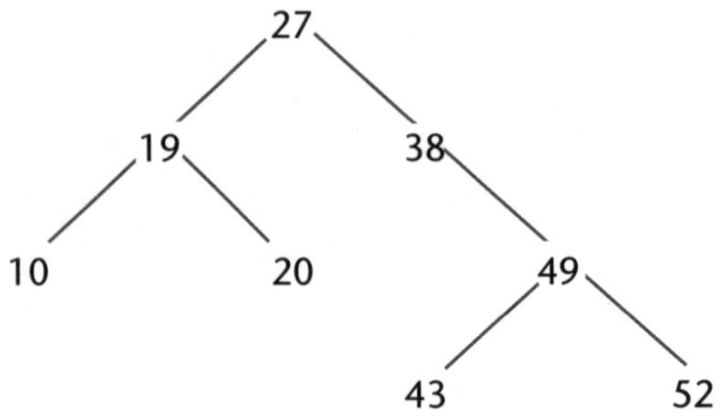

To insert data into an ordered tree the following recursive algorithm can be used:

```
PROCEDURE insert(Tree, Item)
        IF Tree is empty THEN create new tree with Item as the root.
        ELSE    IF Item < Root
                    THEN insert(Left sub-tree of Tree, Item)
                    ELSE insert(Right sub-tree of Tree, Item)
                ENDIF
        ENDIF
ENDPROC
```

Another common use of a binary tree is to hold an algebraic expression, for example:

X + Y * 2

could be stored as:

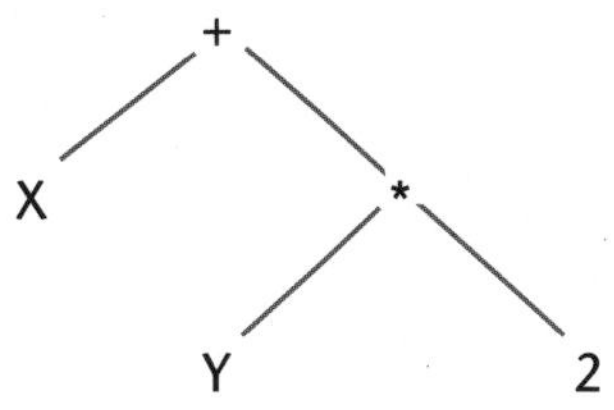

Binary trees can be traversed in three different orders: pre-order, in-order and post-order.

Pre-order traversal

The name pre-order comes from the use of binary trees to store expressions. The pre-order traversal produces the operators before the items. Pre-order is defined as:

- visit the root node
- traverse the left sub-tree
- traverse the right sub-tree.

A procedure to output the tree T in pre-order can be written in pseudocode as:

```
PROCEDURE PREORDER(T)
        PRINT(Contents of the root node)
        PREORDER(Left sub-tree of T)
        PREORDER(Right sub-tree of T)
ENDPROC
```

The result if applied to the tree above is + X * Y 2.

In-order traversal

An in-order traversal will produce an expression in the form that you are used to. The operators come between the items.

An in-order traversal produces the operators between the items and is defined as:

- traverse the left sub-tree
- visit the root node
- traverse the right sub-tree.

Post-order traversal

You may also know post-order as reverse polish.

A post-order traversal places the operators after the items and is defined as:

- traverse the left sub-tree
- traverse the right sub-tree
- visit the root node.

Progress check

1 Write a pseudocode algorithm to represent a procedure PostOrder(Tree) that outputs the contents of a binary tree in post-order.

2 What is the result of applying your algorithm to the following binary tree?

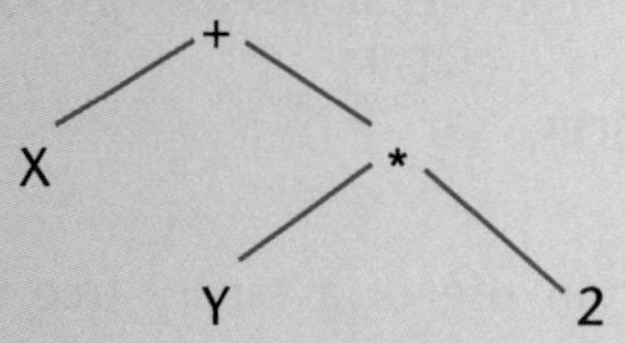

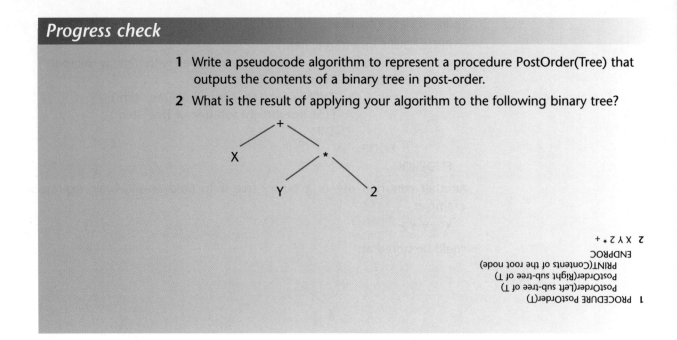

```
1 PROCEDURE PostOrder(T)
  PostOrder(Left sub-tree of T)
  PostOrder(Right sub-tree of T)
  PRINT(Contents of the root node)
  ENDPROC
```

2 X Y 2 * +

7.7 Sorting and searching algorithms

LEARNING SUMMARY

After studying this section you should be able to:

- *understand algorithms to search for an item*
- *describe methods of sorting data*
- *explain how to merge two sets of data*

The different types of sort and search

AQA	M4
EDEXCEL	M5
OCR	M4
WJEC	CP4

Searching algorithms are used to find an item in a list. The algorithm will be given the key of the item to be found and the search will work through the list looking for a match.

Sorting algorithms are used to place a list of items into key sequence (either ascending or descending).

Linear search

A procedure to search an ordered list of items for an item can be performed by starting with the first item and proceeding through the list until the item is found. The search is completed when the item is found or when it comes across an item that has a larger valued key than the required item. An algorithm to search an array Arr might be:

```
PROCEDURE LinearSearch(RequiredItem)
        Found := false
        Failed := false
        Current := 1
        WHILE (Current <= MaxSize) AND (Found = false) AND (Failed = false)
            IF RequiredItem = Arr[Current] THEN Found := true
            ELSE
              IF RequiredItem < Arr[Current] THEN
                Add 1 to Current
                IF Current > MaxSize THEN Failed := true
                ENDIF
              ELSE Failed := true
              ENDIF
            ENDIF
        ENDWHILE
ENDPROC
```

Binary search

A binary search is dramatically faster than a linear search when there are a large number of items.

A linear search requires that, on average, half the items will be inspected. A binary search is more efficient. It operates on the principle that the middle item divides the list into two halves. By inspecting the middle item the program can establish which half contains the required item. The algorithm continues by repeating the process on the half that contains the required item. A pseudocode procedure to perform this process is given below.

Key points from AS

- **Algorithms**
  Revise AS page 110

```
/* Low is the number of the first element in the array and
High is the number of the last element */
PROCEDURE BinarySearch(Low, High, RequiredItem)
        Found := False
        REPEAT
          Middle := Integer part of ((Low + High)/2)
          IF Arr[Middle] = RequiredItem
              THEN Found := true
          ELSE IF Arr[Middle] > RequiredItem
                  THEN High := Middle – 1
              ELSE Low := Middle + 1
              ENDIF
          ENDIF
        UNTIL (Found = True) OR (Low > High)
ENDPROC
```

Merging

Merging can equally apply to sequential files.

It is often necessary to merge two lists of items. This can only be done efficiently if the lists are both in the same sequence. The algorithm is simpler if terminating values that are larger than any value in the lists are added to the end of the lists before the merge takes place. A pseudocode procedure to merge two lists into a third is as follows:

```
PROCEDURE Merge(Arr1,Arr2,Arr3)
        Current1 := 1
        Current2 := 1
        Current3 := 1
        WHILE Arr1[Current1] is not a terminator
            OR Arr2[Current2] is not a terminator do
            IF Arr1[Current1] < Arr2[Current2]
                THEN
                  Arr3[Current3] := Arr1[Current1]
                  Add 1 to Index1
                ELSE
                  Arr3[Current3] := Arr2[Current2]
                  Add 1 to Index2
            ENDIF
            Add 1 to Index3
        ENDWHILE
ENDPROC
```

Bubble sort

The bubble sort is so called as the small numbers bubble slowly to the surface while the large numbers drop like stones to the bottom.

The bubble sort is not very efficient but it is simple to program and a useful algorithm when there are not many items involved. The bubble sort performs a number of passes through the items, each pass putting the items into a slightly better sequence. During a pass the algorithm compares each item with the following item and, if they are out of sequence, it swaps their positions. The effect is shown in Figure 59.

Original list	*After pass 1*	*After pass 2*	*After pass 3*	*After pass 4*	*After pass 5*	*After pass 6*	*After pass 7*
49	24	17	17	17	17	17	15
24	17	24	22	18	18	15	17
17	47	22	18	19	15	18	18
47	22	18	19	15	19	19	19
22	18	19	15	22	22	22	22
18	19	15	24	24	24	24	24
19	15	47	47	47	47	47	47
15	49	49	49	49	49	49	49

Figure 59

The maximum number of passes required to obtain a correct sequence is *N*–1, where *N* is the number of items. The algorithm can be improved by halting if no items are swapped during a pass. This improved algorithm might be:

```
PROCEDURE Bubblesort
        Pass := 1
        REPEAT
            SwapFlag := false
            FOR Count := 1 TO NoOfItems
                IF Arr[Count] > Arr[Count+1] THEN
                  Temp := Arr[Count]
                  Arr[Count] := Arr[Count+1]
                  Arr[Count+1] := Temp
                  SwapFlag := true
                ENDIF
            ENDFOR
            Add 1 to Pass
        UNTIL Pass = NoOfItems OR SwapFlag = false
ENDPROC
```

Insertion sort

The insertion sort is an improvement on the bubble sort but it is still relatively slow and suitable only when there is a limited number of items. The items are copied into a new array one at a time. Each item is inserted in the correct place and all the succeeding items that are already in the new array are moved up one place to make space. It is generally more efficient to start at the end of the list, rather than the start, when inserting.

Quicksort

As its name might suggest, the quicksort is, indeed, very fast. It operates as follows:

1 Select an item at random (often the last item).
2 Create two new lists of items, one with all the items smaller than the chosen item and the other with the rest.
3 Repeat step 1 with each list until the lists have a single item.

You should not be asked to write a quicksort algorithm but you may have to trace one.

Progress check

A table is used to store the barcodes of a number of items available in a shop. The table also stores pointers to the location of the data about each item. The barcodes are stored in a table in numerical order, smallest first.

Give outline algorithms in whatever form you consider appropriate, to:

1 search the table for a specific barcode using a binary search [6]

2 insert a new entry in the table when a new product is offered by the shop. [4]

OCR 2509 Specimen

1 Assume that N is the number of items in the table.

```
High := N
Low := 1
Found := False
While (High>Low) AND (Found=False) do
        Middle := Integer part of (Low+High)/2
        If table[Middle] = barcode then Found:= true
        Else    if table[Middle] > barcode then High := Middle –1
                Else Low := Middle + 1
Endwhile
/* Middle contains location of barcode,
   Found indicates whether barcode was found */
```

2

```
N := position of last barcode in table
StoredFlag := false
REPEAT
    IF Table[N] < barcode THEN
        Insert entry in Table[N+1]
        StoredFlag := true
    ELSE
        Table[N+1] := Table[N]
        Subtract 1 from N
    ENDIF
    IF N=1 THEN
        Insert entry in Table[1]
        StoredFlag := true
    ENDIF
UNTIL StoredFlag = true
```

This algorithm starts at the end of the table and works forwards to improve efficiency.

Sample questions and model answers

1

A routine for manipulating text strings uses the following pre-defined functions:

Len(q) returns the number of characters in the text string q

Right$(q,p) returns a string consisting of the last (rightmost) p characters of the string q

Left$(q,p) returns a string consisting of the first (leftmost) p characters of the string q.

The algorithm for this routine is shown below.

```
string: message, newstring
// main program
input message
newstring := ""
output message
docharacter(message,newstring)
output newstring
// end of program
procedure docharacter(a,outstring) // both parameters passed by reference
    string: piece
    integer: x
    x := Len(a)
    piece := Right$(a,1)
    outstring := outstring + piece
    x := x – 1
    if x > 0 then
        a := Left$(a,x)
        docharacter(a,outstring)
    endif
endproc
```

Trace the algorithm and show what is output if the word CAT is input. [9]

NEAB 1999, CP04

answer overleaf

Sample questions and model answers (continued)

			1st call to docharacter				2nd call to docharacter				3rd call to docharacter				
Instruction	new string	message	a	outstring	x	piece	a	outstring	X	piece	a	outstring	x	piece	Output
input message		CAT													
newstring := “ ”	" "														
output message															CAT
docharacter(message,newstring)			CAT	" "											
x := Len(a)					3										
piece := Right$(a,l)						T									
outstring := outstring + piece				T											
x := x − 1					2										
if x > 0 then															
a:=Left$(a,x)			CA												
docharacter(a, outstring)							CA	T							
x := Len(a)									2						
piece := Right$ (a,1)										A					
outstring := outstring + piece								TA							
x := x − 1									1						
if x > 0 then															
a:=Left$(a,x)							C								
docharacter(a, outstring)											C	TA			
x := Len(a)													1		
piece := Right$(a,1)														C	
outstring := outstring + piece												TAC			
x:= x − 1													0		
if x > 0 then															
endif															
endproc							C	TAC							
endif															
endproc			C	TAC											
endif															
endproc	TAC	C													
output newstring															TAC

Sample questions and model answers (continued)

2

(a) Define the term algorithm. [2]

(a) An algorithm is a finite set of rules to solve a specific problem.

(b) Algorithms are often described using pseudocode. State two other methods of specifying algorithms. [2]

(b) A flowchart could be used. Another method is to write the algorithm in less formal structured English or as a sequence of defined steps.

(c) Programmers sometimes use recursive algorithms.

(i) Describe the key features of a recursive algorithm. [2]

(c) (i) A recursive algorithm is one that calls itself. It must also have a terminating condition to allow it to finish.

(ii) Describe two advantages of a recursive algorithm when available. [2]

Any two will gain you the marks.

(ii) A recursive may be a 'natural' solution, i.e. it may match the problem.

As a result it may be easier to program the solution recursively.

A recursive solution is often very efficient.

(d) The following algorithm is intended to work out the minimum number of coins required to pay any amount of cash up to £4.99, and output a list of the required coins.

(Note: coins of the following type are available: £1 50p 20p 10p 5p 2p 1p. You should assume that there is **no** £2 coin available.)

For instance, for the amount £1.71, the algorithm will correctly output the following:

£1 coin 50p coin 20p coin 1p coin

```
algorithm select_coin;
input (amount_in pounds);
set amount_in_pence = amount in pounds * 100;
if amount_in_pence >= 100 then
    output "£1 coin ";
    set amount_in_pence = amount_in_pence – 100;
endif;
if amount_in_pence >= 50 then
    output "50p coin ";
    set amount_in_pence = amount in pence – 50;
endif;
if amount_in_pence >= 20 then
    output "20p coin ";
    set amount_in_pence = amount in pence – 20;
endif;
if amount_in_pence >= 10 then
output "10p coin ";
    set amount_in_pence = amount_in_pence – 10;
endif;
if amount_in_pence >= 5 then
    output "5p coin ";
    set amount_in_pence = amount in pence – 5;
```

Sample questions and model answers (continued)

```
endif;
if amount_in_pence >= 2 then
    output "2p coin ";
    set amount_in_pence = amount_in pence – 2;
endif;
if amount_in pence >= 1 then output "1p coin ".
```

This algorithm will not work correctly for every amount up to £4.99.

(i) Write down the output of this algorithm resulting from an input of

(I) £1.33 [2]

(d) (i) (I) £1 coin 20p coin 10p coin 2p coin 1p coin

(II) £2.44

(II) £1 coin 50p coin 20p coin 10p coin 5p coin 2p coin 1p coin

(ii) To correct the algorithm, it is necessary to make one change concerning the number of £1 coins output, and also a similar change relating to two other coins. Write down the two other coins. [1]

(ii) 20p coin and 2p coin

(iii) Copy and amend part of the algorithm so that the correct number of £1 coins is output. (You do not need to consider the other coins you mentioned in part (ii.) [4]

WJEC Specimen CP4

(iii)
```
while amount_in_pence >= 100 then
    output "£1 coin ";
    set amount_in_pence = amount_in_pence - 100;
endwhile;
```

Practice examination questions

1

An algebraic expression is represented in a binary tree as follows:

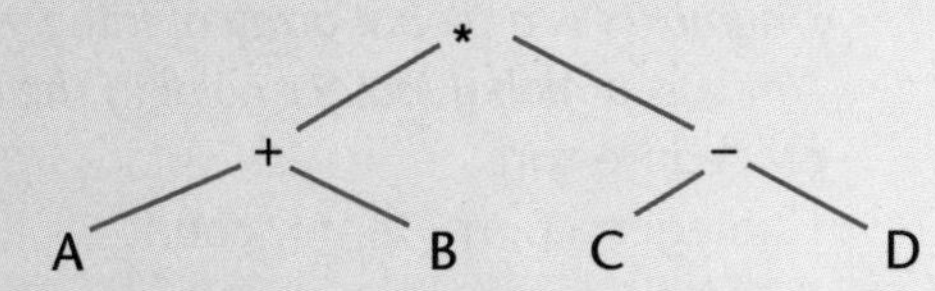

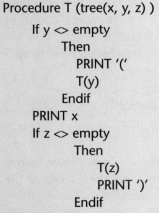

(a) Using a copy of this tree, label its *root*, a *branch* and a *leaf*. [3]

(b) On the same copy, mark and label the *left sub-tree* and the *right sub-tree* of this tree. [2]

A recursively defined procedure T, which takes a tree structure, tree(x, y, z) as its single parameter, where x is the root, y is the left sub-tree and z is the right sub-tree, is defined below (<> means not equal to).

```
Procedure T (tree(x, y, z) )
    If y <> empty
        Then
            PRINT '('
            T(y)
        Endif
    PRINT x
    If z <> empty
        Then
            T(z)
            PRINT ')'
        Endif
EndProc
```

(c) What is meant by *recursively defined*? [1]

(d) Explain why a stack is necessary in order to execute procedure T recursively. [3]

(e) Dry-run the following procedure call:

```
T (   tree( '*', tree ('+', tree ('A', empty, empty), tree ( 'B', empty, empty ) ),
      tree ( '-', tree ('C', empty, empty), tree ( 'D', empty, empty) )
              )
       )
```

showing clearly the PRINTed output and the values of the parameter omitted from the table (rows 4, 5, 6, 7) for the **seven** calls of T.

Call number	*Parameter*
1	tree('*', tree('+', tree('A',empty,empty), tree('B',empty,empty)),
	tree('-', tree('C',empty,empty), tree('D',empty,empty))
	)
2	tree('+',tree('A',empty,empty), tree('B',empty,empty))
3	tree('A',empty,empty)
4	
5	
6	
7	

[10]

(f) What tree traversal algorithm does procedure T describe? [1]

AEB 1999, Paper 3

Practice examination questions (continued)

2

The algorithm below shows a procedure called *sort*.

```
//numbers is a global array of integers
//max is a global integer holding the number of values to be sorted
procedure sort
   integer: cp, rp, temp, count
   rp:=1
   repeat
         rp := rp+1
         cp := 1
         while rp > cp do
            if numbers [rp] > numbers [cp] then
               temp := numbers[rp]
               for count := rp to cp + 1 step –1
                    numbers [count] := numbers[count –1]
               endfor
               numbers [cp] := temp
            endif
            cp := cp+1
         endwhile
   until rp = max
endproc
```

(a) Using the column headings shown below, trace the algorithm for the procedure sort when the array numbers contains the values 13, 25, 24 and max = 3.

Comment	Count	rp	max	cp	temp	Numbers		
						1	2	3
Global values on call			3			13	25	24

[10]

(b) Name the sort method used in the algorithm above. [1]

(c) Why would this method be inefficient if the array numbers contained 500 values? [2]

NEAB 2000, CP04

3

Describe, using pseudocode or otherwise, an efficient algorithm to merge two lists of integers which are stored in ascending order of magnitude. [5]

EDEXCEL 1999, Paper 2

Chapter 8

Systems development

The following topics are covered in this chapter:

- *Systems analysis*
- *System design*
- *System implementation*
- *Project management*

8.1 Systems analysis

After studying this section you should be able to:

- *describe fact-finding techniques*
- *explain reporting techniques*
- *evaluate the volumes of data*

LEARNING SUMMARY

Techniques and procedures

AQA	M5, M6
EDEXCEL	M5, M6
OCR	M5, M6
WJEC	CP6

These techniques should be familiar from AS. You will be expected to identify the best method at A Level.

Fact-finding techniques

There are a number of methods of collecting information including:

- inspecting records
- observing current practice
- interviewing
- questionnaires.

Inspecting current records and observing current practice will give a good idea of the way things are actually done, rather than the way things are supposed to be done.

Interviewing staff is a very effective way to gather information about the system but it is very time-consuming.

Questionnaires must be well thought out. The questions must be precise and the questionnaire should be no longer than is absolutely necessary if it is to be effective. It is a very efficient method of collecting a lot of data if you can be sure that the questionnaires have been filled in with care and attention. There is a danger that most of them will be put in the bin.

Reporting the findings

The fact-finding will produce a large amount of information that needs to be reported. Some of the methods of reporting the current system are described below.

System flowcharts

Used to describe the sequence of processes in a system (see AS Guide section 7.2).

Entity attribute relationship diagramming (EAR)

A conceptual model of the data identifying the entities and attributes and showing how these relate together. The result is an entity-relationship model as described in Chapter 5, section 5.3 on relational databases.

Key points from AS

- **The systems life cycle** *Revise AS pages 92–93*
- **Analysis** *Revise AS pages 93–96*

Data dictionary

This stores details of the data used. Typical information includes:

- the name of the data item
- the type of data stored
- the amount of storage required for each data item
- who owns the data
- who can access the data
- which programs use the data.

Each relational database will have its own data dictionary (see section 5.3 Relational Databases).

Data flow diagram (DFD)

An alternative method of documenting the flow of data through a system is a data flow diagram (DFD).

A data flow diagram concentrates on the flow of data. Typical data flow diagram symbols are:

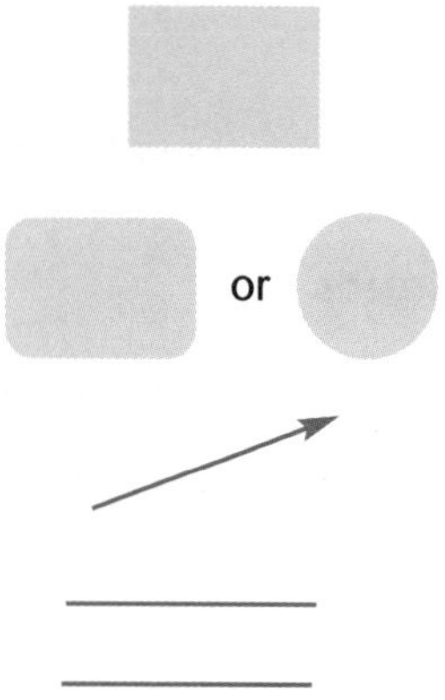

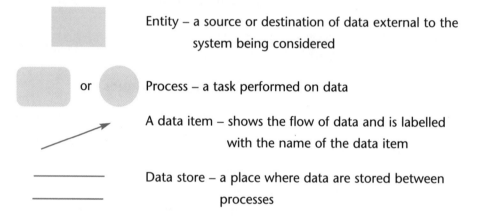

Entity – a source or destination of data external to the system being considered

Process – a task performed on data

A data item – shows the flow of data and is labelled with the name of the data item

Data store – a place where data are stored between processes

A system to accept orders online and to create valid orders on magnetic disk and an error report on the printer might be shown in a data flow diagram like Figure 60.

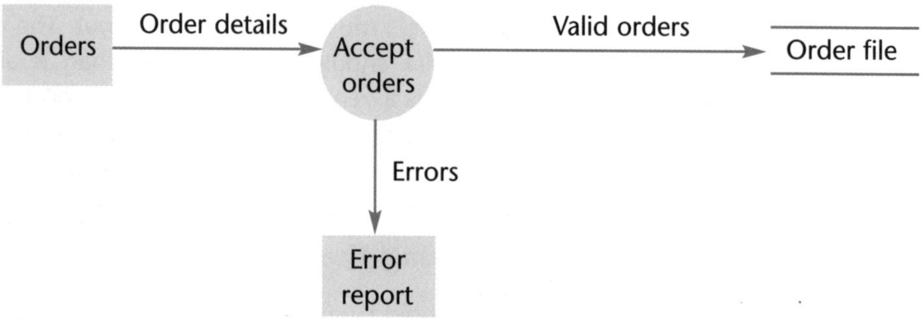

Figure 60

The DFD concentrates on the flow of data. The system flowchart concentrates on the processes involved.

Evaluating volumes of data

It is important to establish the amount and type of data involved in any system. This study should take into account:

- the number of forms and reports that are involved in the system
- the amount of data and the types of data that are contained
- how often the data has to be processed
- the type of processing involved, for example online or batch.

A general term for the amount of data and the characteristics of the users is **volumetrics**.

Progress check

Three methods of obtaining information about an existing system are:

1 observation
2 interviewing staff
3 questionnaires.

For each of the above give **one** advantage over the other methods.

1 An accurate picture of the actual operation of the current system will be obtained, rather than the documented processes.
2 The operation of the system can be examined in detail.
3 An efficient method of obtaining a large amount of information.

8.2 System design

After studying this section you should be able to:

- *explain prototyping*
- *explain user interface design*
- *describe how to ensure the security of a system*
- *explain disaster planning*

LEARNING SUMMARY

Design techniques and system security

AQA	M5, M6
EDEXCEL	M5, M6
OCR	M5, M6
WJEC	CP4, CP5, CP6

Most of these will be familiar from AS. The difference will be that you should be capable of using them rather than being familiar with them.

Having obtained as much information as possible about the current system the process of designing the new system can now take place. There are a number of techniques to help with this task, such as:

- system flowcharts – see above
- data flow diagrams (DFD) – see above
- entity attribute relationship diagrams (EAR) – see above
- prototyping – see AS Guide section 7.3, Design
- user interface design – see AS Guide section 7.3, Design
- structure diagrams – see AS Guide section 7.3, Design
- pseudocode – see Chapter 7 Algorithms.

Security

It is vital that data are kept securely and that they are not damaged or lost. The risks include:

- hardware failure
- fire
- theft
- disgruntled employees
- hackers trying to break into the system
- computer viruses.

Key points from AS

- **Design**
  Revise AS pages 97–99
- **Security**
  Revise AS page 87

You should be careful to determine the risk and then apply the *appropriate* solution.

The methods to counteract these risks include the following.

- Backups – important data should be backed up and at least one copy should be stored in either a fireproof safe or an alternative location in case of fire.
- Physical security – areas at risk must be secure with locks, security cameras, security guards as appropriate.
- Passwords on online systems to prevent unauthorised access to the system.
- Employee checks:
  - ID cards to check employees
  - careful vetting before employees are signed on
  - instant removal of access rights to sacked employees
  - separation of tasks to prevent collusion to commit fraud between employees
  - use of passwords to limit access to certain parts of the system
  - educating staff to be aware of breaches of security.
- Anti-virus software should be installed and all disks that are brought into the company need to be checked to prevent a virus attack.
- Consider appointing a security manager and appropriate software to allow access to all terminals to observe exactly what is being entered.
- An online system must maintain a log file of all transactions. This will allow the updates since the last backup to be reprocessed in the case of hardware failure.

Remember that you can have a hierarchy of passwords.

Progress check

An online system suffers a hard-disk failure in the middle of a day's trading.

(a) Explain how the files can be recovered.

(b) Explain what should be done while the recovery is taking place.

1 The last backup should be copied on to another hard disk. The log file should be used to update the master file.

2 While the recovery takes place the master file will not be available but the system could be maintained at a lower level of service. Any transactions could be logged and used to update the master file when the system is up and running.

8.3 System implementation

LEARNING SUMMARY

After studying this section you should be able to:

- *describe system conversion*
- *describe testing strategies for the development of a system*
- *explain training needs*
- *describe the requirements for manuals*
- *explain system evaluation*
- *describe system maintenance*

Implementation procedure and testing

AQA	M5, M6
EDEXCEL	M5, M6
OCR	M5, M6
WJEC	CP4, CP6

If the system is modular in nature it can be implemented one module at a time.

Key points from AS

- **Analysis** *Revise AS page 92*

There are a number of stages in the implementation of a new system.

- Testing – see below.
- Conversion – there are two main approaches (see AS Guide, page 95).
  - implement the system in parts (for example department by department)
  - dual-run the new system alongside the old system.
- Training – the users of the new system will need to be trained in its use.
- Evaluation – a post-implementation review will take place after a period has elapsed to allow the system to 'settle down'. It should involve:
  - comparing the actual performance with the anticipated performance
  - known bugs in the system
  - unexpected benefits of the system
  - unexpected problems with the system.
- Maintenance – this will be ongoing (described in AS Guide, page 96).

Testing strategies

There are various strategies for testing. The first tests will involve the testing of the programs. The approaches include various modules individually.

- Top-down – the program will be tested with limited functionality. Most functions will be replaced with stubs that contain no code. Functions are gradually added to the program until the complete program is tested.
- Bottom-up – each function is tested individually. They can then be combined to test the complete program.
- Black-box testing – the program is regarded as a black box and is tested according to its specification. No account is taken of the way the program is written.
- White-box testing – each path through the program is tested. This method ensures that all lines of code are tested.

A famous integration failure was the space shuttle. The various parts were tested but they failed to communicate with each other when they were installed in the shuttle.

Once the programs are tested they can be installed and the analyst can test the system. System testing can involve:

- unit testing – testing each program individually
- integration testing – testing the complete system.

Progress check

This is a typical question where you must use common sense to apply your knowledge. Any answer that shows that you have thought about the problem is likely to get you some marks.

Briefly describe **three** criteria you would use in the evaluation of a computer-based solution. [3]

NEAB 1999, CP04

Any **three** of the following: Can it carry out all the required tasks? Is it easy to use? Is the system easily maintainable? Is the system compatible with existing systems? Is it better than the previous system? Is it cost effective?

8.4 Project management

After studying this section you should be able to:

- *describe the process of project management*
- *explain the use of Gantt charts*
- *explain the use of critical path analysis*

LEARNING SUMMARY

Project Evaluation and Review Technique

EDEXCEL M5
OCR M6
WJEC CP6

Controlling a software project is no different from scheduling any project involving a number of personnel, so general-purpose project management methods can be used. Probably the most popular method is known as PERT (Project Evaluation and Review Technique) and there are a number of PERT software packages available. The technique involves breaking a project up into a number of separate activities. It is now possible to state the order in which these activities have to be performed, for example a program must be coded before it is tested. The activities are all interconnected into a PERT network. Figure 61 is a simple example of a PERT network to develop a program that comprises three parts (A, B and C). Each part can be developed separately.

Some packages will place the activities in boxes and indicate the dependencies by the arrows, but the method is the same in principle.

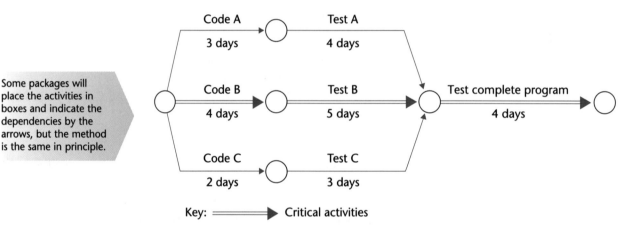

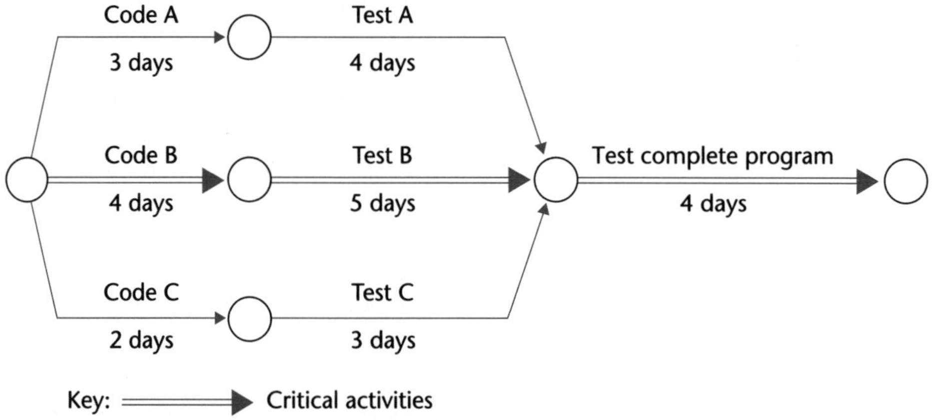

Figure 61

PERT uses a technique known as critical path method to identify how long it will take to complete the project and which activities are critical, i.e. which activities must not be delayed if the project is to finish on time. All the activities that are critical are known as the critical path.

A method of showing when activities take place is known as a Gantt chart. Figure 62 is a Gantt chart showing the project described above.

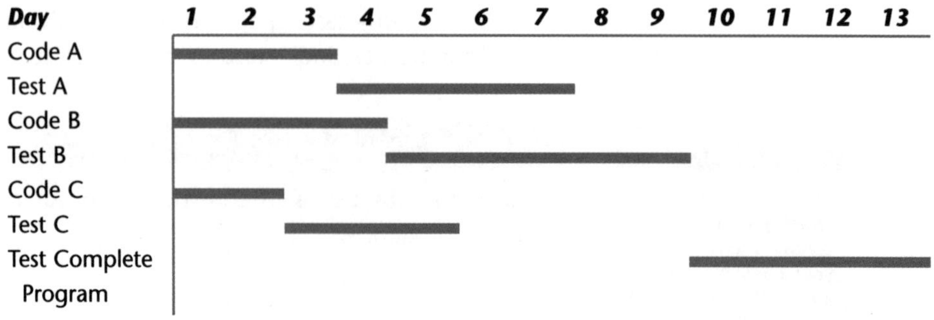

Figure 62

Progress check

A team of computing specialists has been given the task of designing, coding and implementing software for some of the information systems in a garage.

Identify two methods which could be employed to control the costs within this project. For each method state the activities which could be controlled. [4]

EDEXCEL Specimen Test 5

Gantt charting could be used to control the employment of the computing specialists within the project.

Critical path analysis could be used to control the sequencing of tasks within the project.

Sample questions and model answers

1

During system development a *data flow diagram* may be used to represent all or part of the system. Below is an outline of a data flow diagram for a system to produce gas bills where meter readings, having been recorded using a hand-held device, are processed against the customer master file to produce the printed gas bills for the customers and a printed error report.
Give an appropriate label to **each** of the numbered elements **A** to E.

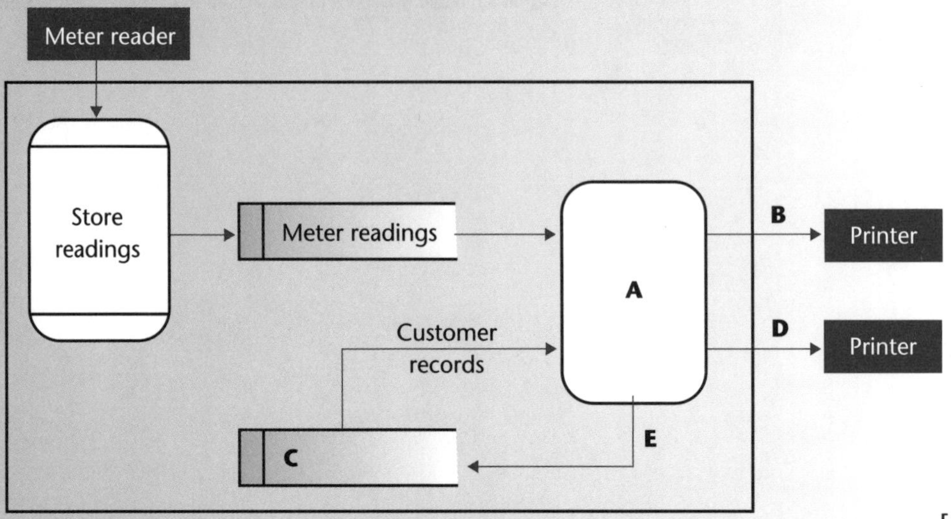

[5]

AEB 1998, Paper 2

B and D can be interchanged.

A Calculate bills
B Gas bills
C Customer file
D Error report
E Updated records

2

A system for the production of about one hundred thousand electricity bills per day is required. A number of alternative systems are available for purchase.
The following features of each alternative system have been given numerical weightings to reflect their relative importance:

Feature	Weighting
A: purchase cost	5
B: maintenance and running costs	10
C: user friendliness of the software	3
D: bill printing speed	12
E: quality of printed output	8

The required system is selected as follows:

Sample questions and model answers (continued)

Step 1	Rank each feature of each alternative system in reverse order of merit.	
Step 2	Multiply each of these rankings by its respective weighting.	
Step 3	For each alternative system calculate the total of these computed values. The system with the largest total should be selected.	

(a) Suggest **three** possible consequences of feature C's being given a low weighting. [3]

(a) The consequences include:
The system could be difficult to use.
The operators and users will need to have been well trained.
The documentation for the operators and users will have to be extensive.

(b) Comment on the relative size of the weighting given to feature D in comparison to the other features. [2]

(b) The bill printing speed is the most important feature as one hundred thousand bills are required each day.

(c) State **three** advantages of this method of selecting a computer system. [3]

(c) The advantages include:
The evaluations are objective.
The evaluations are consistent.
The method can be applied to any application.

(d) Identify **five** factors other than those listed which should be taken into account before a system is purchased. Justify your suggestions. [10]

(d) The factors could be:
The robustness of the hardware as the system is to be heavily used.
The user support available from the vendor as breakdowns need to be rectified quickly.
The effectiveness of the system as the output needs to be accurate and consistent.
The convenience of implementing the system as the changeover needs to be seamless.
The level of training required as this could have an effect on staffing
The capability for expansion as the number of customers might increase.
Compatibility with other in-house systems as the new system will have to fit into the data processing facilities of the company.
The trade record of the suppliers as the system needs to be reliable.
The need for working in teams and the roles of the people involved as this has a consequence for recruitment of staff.

You need to provide five valid factors and corresponding reasons.

EDEXCEL Specimen Test 5

Practice examination questions

1 The Museum of the Late Twentieth Century (MOLT) has built up a collection of objects intended to help to serve as reminders to future generations of important matters in the last two decades of the second millennium. It has many mechanical, electronic and image-based materials including interactive video as well as more conventional films and music.

MOLT is still expanding its collection, and is moving to new premises. It is planning what facilities and information services it should make available to users of the museum, both visiting and remote.

MOLT is anxious to ensure that its layout in its new premises meets the interests of its users. It decides to build a traffic flow simulation of the movement of visitors along the various routes between the exhibits. They have no previous in-house experience of simulation.

(a) Explain how MOLT might use simulation in the process of prototyping its new layout. [4]

(b) Discuss the different approaches which MOLT might use to produce the simulation and their relative advantages and disadvantages in this context. [4]

(c) State what outputs you would expect the simulation to display and describe the ways in which the information might suitably be presented. [4]

(d) Identify the main features of a testing strategy for the simulation. [4]

OCR 2511 Specimen

2 State **two** reasons for performing a design review during software development. [2]

NEAB 1998, CP04

3 A farmer has converted some outbuildings into several identical apartments. The apartments will be let to holiday makers for periods of one or more weeks from midday Saturday to midday Saturday. The farmer wishes to have a computer application program to help with the letting process. It should be possible to:

Input a date and determine which apartments are available to be let.
Reserve an apartment for a particular week or weeks and record the customer details.
Produce letters to confirm bookings for customers who have paid a deposit.
Print schedules at the end of each week to inform cleaners which apartments need cleaning.
Generate periodic reports for accounting and taxation purposes.

The application is to be based on three files: a Property File, a Customer File and a Bookings File.

(a) Identify the record structure of the three files, paying particular attention to the key field and the way in which the files will be linked. [9]

(b) The user interface screen will have named icons that can be selected by clicking with the mouse. Design a suitable interface screen. [3]

(c) Briefly describe one of the periodic reports which the farmer will require and indicate the processing needed to generate it. [3]

EDEXCEL 1998, Paper 1

Chapter 9

Networking

The following topics are covered in this chapter:

- *Data communication principles*
- *Local area networks*
- *Wide area networks*
- *Common protocols*

9.1 Data communication principles

After studying this section you should be able to:

- *describe the media used for data transmission*
- *explain what is meant by simplex, half-duplex and full-duplex*
- *explain what is meant by the terms 'baseband' and 'broadband'*
- *describe synchronous data transmission*
- *describe error detection methods*
- *describe error correction methods*
- *explain what is meant by data compression*
- *explain what is meant by data encryption*

LEARNING SUMMARY

Data transmission

AQA	M5
EDEXCEL	M4
OCR	M6
WJEC	CP5

Transmission media

Data can be transmitted electrically using copper wire. The wire can be in a number of different layouts:

- open wires – ribbon cable is an example of open wires
- coaxial cable with a signal wire surrounded by a wire mesh
- twisted pair cable.

Another option is to use optical fibres. An optical fibre uses light signals that can be turned on and off to represent the data bits. It is also possible to use wireless transmission using:

- radio waves
- infra-red.

The use of mobile phones is an increasingly popular means of transmission.

Three characteristics of the way that data is transmitted and received are:

- simplex – transmission in one direction only
- half-duplex – transmission in both directions but only one direction at any one moment in time
- full-duplex – transmission in both directions simultaneously.

Baseband

When data bits are transmitted as square waves this is known as baseband transmission (see Figure 63).

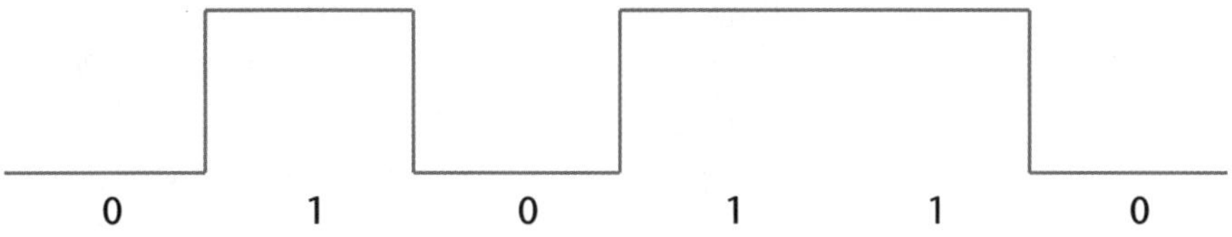

Figure 63

Key points from AS

- **Data transmission**
  Revise AS pages 64–68

Broadband transmission rates are normally greater than 30 Mbps.

Broadband

Data can be encoded into analogue waves using the complete range of possible frequencies available. In this case the transmission is called broadband. Broadband transmission provides a much faster transfer rate.

Synchronous data transmission

Synchronous data transmission is used when there is a regular supply of bits to be transmitted. The data bits are transmitted continuously in large blocks. Between the blocks of data, synchronising characters (known as SYN characters) are transmitted (Figure 64).

A synchronous transmission channel transmits SYN characters when there are no data to be transmitted.

Data	SYN characters	Data	SYN characters	Data

Figure 64

Error detection

Four methods of error detection are:

- echo checks
- parity bits
- check sums
- cyclic redundancy check (CRC).

An echo check involves the data that are transmitted being returned to the sender. The sender checks that the returned data are the same as the data that were transmitted.

A parity bit can be attached to each message that is sent. The parity bit check is limited in that it can guarantee only to check for single-bit errors.

A check sum can be added to each message. This can be a simple sum of, say, the number of ones transmitted.

You do not need to worry about the details of polynomial check sums. The calculation of these is outside the syllabus.

A cyclic redundancy check involves the calculation of a polynomial check sum that is added to each message. This check is very efficient at establishing almost all errors that can occur.

Error correction

As well as codes that detect errors there are a number of codes that are able to not only detect but also to correct the error that has occurred. These involve a larger overhead than error detection codes and so they are not so popular. One such error correction code is a **hamming code**.

Data compression

Data compression is used to reduce the amount of data that needs to be transmitted. There are various methods available. Examples are:

- Text can be analysed to look for repetitions of phrases. The phrases can be replaced by single non-printable bytes.
- Delta compression is used on moving pictures. The parts of the picture that change are identified and only the changes are transmitted.
- Lossy compression techniques remove some of the detail, for example, sound can be stored using fewer bits per sample with an appropriate loss of quality.

Common standards for data compression are:

Data compression is particularly useful when transmitting video as this medium requires a very high data transfer rate.

- JPEG (Joint Photographic Expert Group) has defined standards for still picture compression.
- MPEG (Motion Picture Expert Group) has defined standards for moving images.
- MP3 (the Audio Layer 3 of MPEG1) is a popular compression technique for audio.

Data encryption

Data coded in such a way that they make no sense are said to be encrypted. It is often necessary to encrypt data when they are transmitted over a network so that the contents are kept secret. There is a possibility that hackers might be able to read the data that are transmitted but, if the data are encrypted, the contents will be meaningless. The original message is known as plaintext and the encrypted data as ciphertext (see Figure 65).

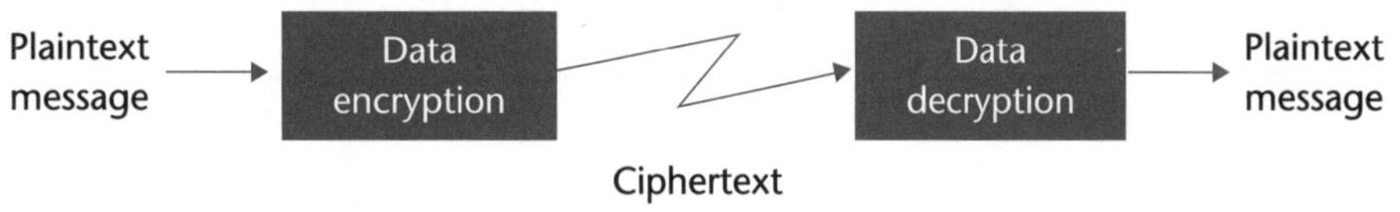

The secure socket layer (SSL) provides a standard method of encryption to allow e-commerce over the Internet.

Figure 65

A common method of encrypting data is to use a standard algorithm that is well known to perform the encryption but to use a secret key. The key is essential to decrypt the message and this must be kept secret.

Progress check

Data can be transmitted using synchronous or asynchronous protocols. Explain when you would use:

1 synchronous transmission

2 asynchronous transmission.

1 When data bits are supplied at a regular rate.

2 When transmissions are irregular.

9.2 Local area networks

After studying this section you should be able to:

- *describe various LAN topologies*
- *understand the use of bridges and gateways*
- *describe asynchronous transfer mode (ATM)*
- *describe polling*
- *describe the use of routers*
- *explain the use of peer-to-peer networks*

LEARNING SUMMARY

LAN configurations

AQA	M5
EDEXCEL	M4
OCR	M6
WJEC	CP5

Carrier sense multiple access

A carrier sense multiple access (CSMA) network will normally use a bus architecture (Figure 66), and the best known CSMA network is known as ethernet.

Figure 66

The protocol states that all computers must sense the carrier (i.e. the bus) at all times. When a computer wishes to transmit, it can do so immediately if it cannot detect any data on the bus. If there are data being transmitted then the computer has to try again later. Sometimes two (or more) computers will start transmitting at the same time. If this happens we say that a collision occurs. When a collision occurs it will be detected by the computers that are transmitting and they will have to stop transmitting and try again later. If the network is heavily loaded there will be many collisions and the performance will deteriorate.

Token ring

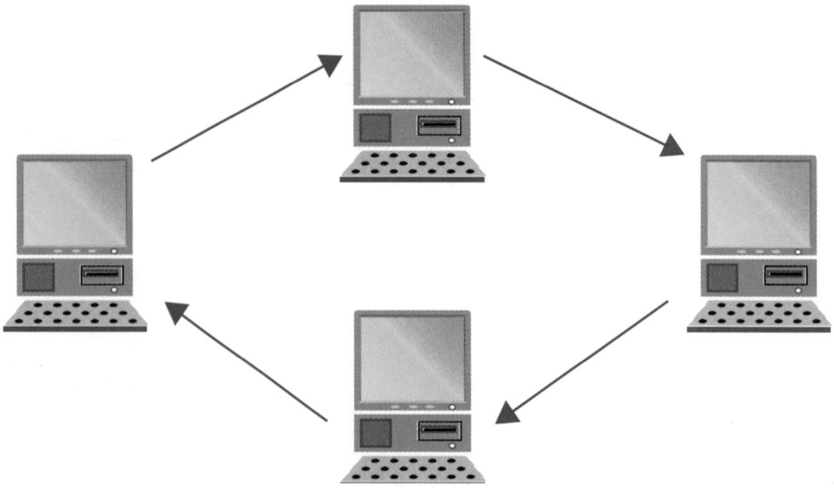

Figure 67

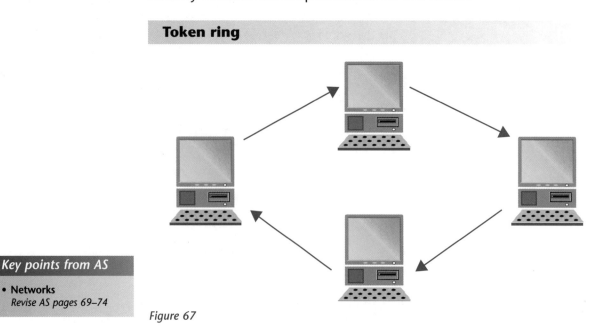

Key points from AS

- **Networks**
  Revise AS pages 69–74

In a token ring, one of the computers generates a token and sends it around the ring (Figure 67). The token ring protocol states that computers cannot transmit until they receive a free token (a free token is one that does not have any data attached). When a free token is received the computer attaches the data and sends it around the ring. The protocol also states that the receiving computer has to return an acknowledgement to state that the data were received. When the sender receives the acknowledgement it must pass on a free token. As there are no collisions this form of LAN allows high-speed transmission.

Star networks

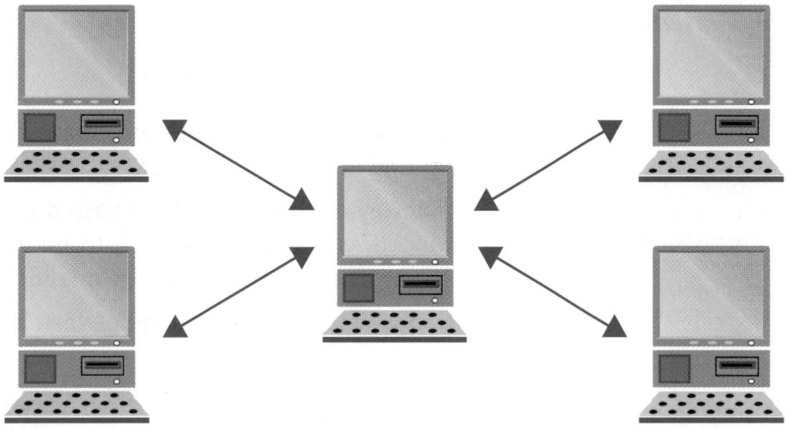

Figure 68

A star network will have a computer at the centre of the star running an operating system that controls the network (Figure 68). This computer will go to each workstation in turn to discover whether it has data to be transmitted. This process is known as polling.

Hubs and routers

A large organisation may well need many computing devices to be connected to the network. This may generate a large amount of traffic. A common solution is to implement a high-speed backbone network. This high-speed backbone may well be some form of ring using optical fibre as a transmission medium. The computers on this backbone are often called routers, as they route the messages to carry on around the network or they divert them to one of the devices attached to the router. Attached to each router there will be one or more computing devices. Figure 69 is an example of such a network

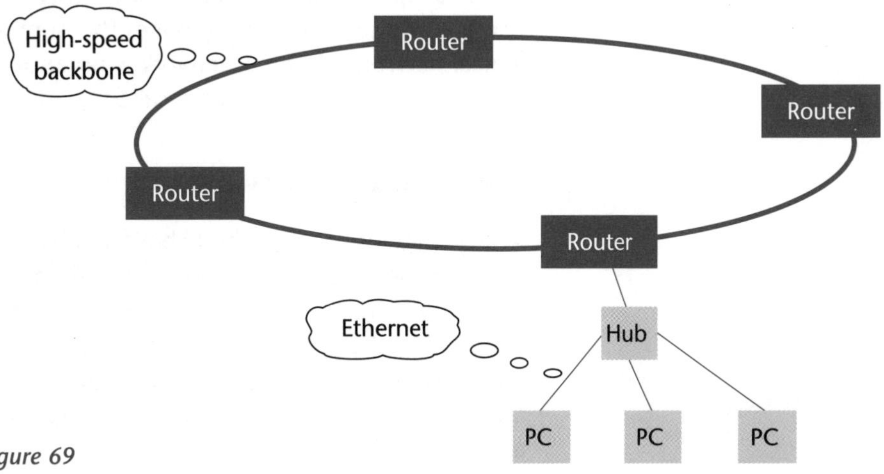

Figure 69

A typical transmission rate for the high-speed network might be 155–622 Mbps (megabits per second). In contrast, ethernet may be 10 or 100 Mbps.

The example shows a high-speed backbone and one of the slower-speed networks that are connected to it. The high-speed backbone may well use asynchronous transfer mode (ATM) as its protocol. ATM divides the data into small, fixed-length packets, known as cells, which are transmitted asynchronously and reassembled at the destination, and provides high-speed data transmission. This is particularly suitable for transmitting continuous audio and video.

There are two standard speeds for ethernet. The connection between the hub and the router is likely to be a high-speed ethernet connection.

The one slower network shown in Figure 69 is a star network with a hub at its centre. When a star is used in this way the computer at its centre is merely acting as a message processor and is known as a hub. You will also notice that the connections are labelled as ethernet. This is a popular way of connecting computers to a network as ethernet network cards are low priced and, when used in this way, do not suffer from collisions.

Bridges and gateways

Bridges and gateways perform similar tasks in that they enable data to be passed from one network to another.

A gateway often gives access to a totally different type of network, for example you may have a gateway to the Internet.

A gateway enables data to be passed to another network that is using a different protocol. As the data will have to be in a different format for each network the gateway converts the data from one format to another.

A bridge acts as a connection between two LANs and makes it appear as if the two networks are one.

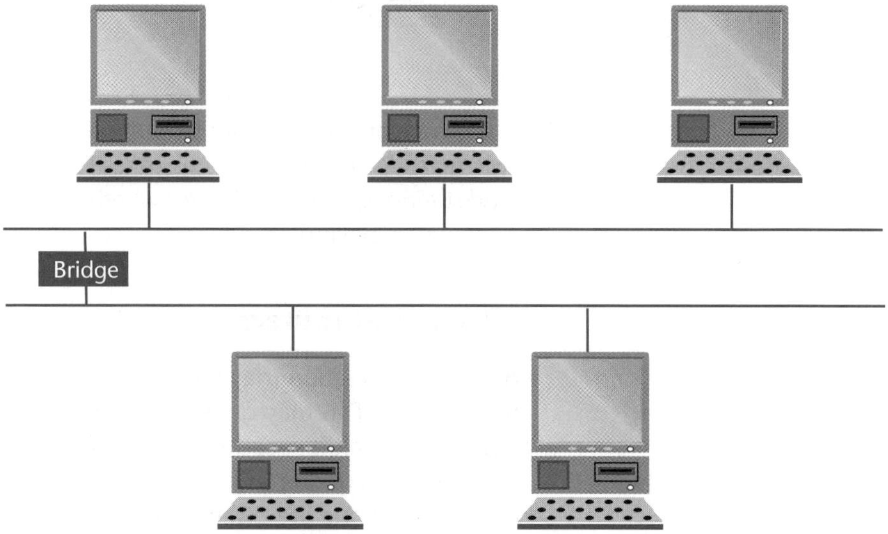

Figure 70

In Figure 70 the bridge makes the two bus networks into one logical network. When a bus network becomes large there is a greater problem with collisions. Using a bridge in this way reduces the number of collisions but maintains a large logical network. When a network is organised into sub-networks using bridges in this way, the sub-networks are called **segments**.

Peer-to-peer networks

A large network as described above will have a number of servers providing all the necessary services that are required. When a small number of computers need to be connected and security is not an issue, another approach is to use peer-to-peer networking. Peer-to-peer networks simply attach computers to a LAN and make the facilities of each computer available to any other computer on the LAN. This is a cheap and simple way of allowing different computers to share resources, such as printers, files and so on.

Progress check

1 Give **one** advantage of a token ring network over a CSMA.

2 Give an example of where **each** would be used.

1 Faster data transmission.

2 CSMA would be used in any environment that has a low data transfer rate, i.e. any example where devices need to transfer limited amounts of data.
Token ring will be used where data transfer rate is high, e.g. for a backbone or any situation where large amounts of data are to be transferred.

9.3 Wide area networks

After studying this section you should be able to:

- *explain circuit switching*
- *explain packet switching*

LEARNING SUMMARY

WAN operation

AQA	M5
EDEXCEL	M4
OCR	M6
WJEC	CP5

A wide area network (WAN) consists of a number of nodes that are connected by long distance communication links called channels (see Figure 71). A channel will normally be one of:

- Telephone line – using a modem the telephone system can be used but it is limited in speed
- ISDN – integrated services digital network lines can be provided that will transmit both data and speech along the same communication links. These links are much faster and operate digitally so speech has to be digitised before it is transmitted.

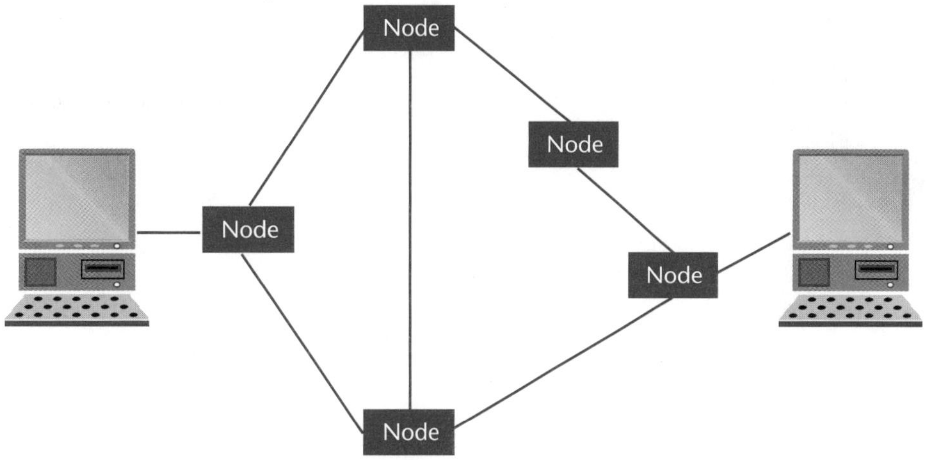

Figure 71

The role of a node is to direct any data along the correct channel.

Key points from AS

- **5.2 Networks**
  Revise AS page 69

Packet switching

Data are transmitted in standard chunks called packets. A packet contains the following information:

- the destination address (where the data are to go to)
- the sender's address (where the data have come from)
- a packet number (used to reassemble messages that have been split up to fit into packets)
- the data.

A datagram is often compared to a letter. You post a letter in a postbox and rely on the Post Office to deliver it.

In a packet switching system, packets (often called **datagrams**) are sent individually through the network. The role of the node is to direct each packet individually. From time to time some channels may become very busy (we say that they are congested) and the nodes are intelligent enough to direct the packets around these busy routes. This means that packets may arrive out of sequence and may need to be reassembled by the receiver.

Circuit switching

This is rather like making a telephone call. You dial the number and the telephone exchanges create a circuit that you can use to speak to the person at the other end.

A circuit switching system uses a different approach to routing. The system uses special packets known as virtual circuit set-up packets. A virtual circuit set-up packet is sent through the network to create a virtual circuit. Once the virtual circuit is created it acts as if there were a single channel through the network and packets can be sent along it.

The virtual circuit cannot benefit from rerouting packets around congestion but there will be no need for the receiver to reassemble messages as the packets will arrive in the correct sequence.

Progress check

1 Give one advantage of circuit switching over packet switching.

2 Give one advantage of packet switching over circuit switching.

1 Packets arrive in the correct sequence.
2 Packets can be routed around congestion, leading to greater throughput.

9.4 Common protocols

After studying this section you should be able to:

- *describe the OSI seven-layer model*
- *describe the TCP/IP protocol stack*
- *describe the history of the Internet*
- *describe FTP (file transfer protocol)*
- *describe HTTP (hyper-text transfer protocol)*
- *describe hypertext mark-up language (HTML)*
- *describe XML (extensible mark-up language)*
- *explain the use of Javascript and applets.*

LEARNING SUMMARY

The various protocols

AQA	M5
EDEXCEL	M4
OCR	M6
WJEC	CP5

OSI seven-layer model

The International Standards Organisation has produced a seven-layer model for open systems intercommunication (OSI) to allow computers of different origins to be connected together. The concept is that suppliers can produce hardware or software to implement any of the seven layers and that other suppliers can provide the other layers. The seven layers are:

7	Application	Network applications such as data transfer, messaging, operating system functions, etc.
6	Presentation	Data transformation (e.g. ASCII to Unicode), data encryption and compression, etc.
5	Session	Establishes and maintains session dialogues (e.g. login session, file transfer sessions)
4	Transport	Provides naming facilities and error correction for inter-network communication
3	Network	Routing through networks
2	Data link	Provides error correction
1	Physical	Standards for electrical connections, bit rates, etc.

You will find that many products cover several layers of the OSI model.

At each layer additional information is added to allow the service to be provided. A layered model in this form is called a protocol stack.

TCP/IP

The TCP/IP protocol stack has similar protocols that effectively implement layers 3 and 4 of the OSI model. IP (Internet protocol) provides level 3 and TCP (transport control protocol) provides level 4.

The Internet

The history of the Internet

Key points from AS

- **Networks**
  Revise AS pages 69–74

By the late 1960s, the US Department of Defense became interested in using computer networks. Through the Advanced Research Projects Agency (ARPA), the military funded research on networking using a variety of technologies. By the late 1970s, ARPA had developed a wide area network called ARPANET that used TCP/IP protocols. From its inception, the Internet project aspired to produce an open system that permitted computers from all vendors to communicate. The open philosophy meant that researchers published all discoveries about the Internet and all specifications needed to build TCP/IP software.

By 1982, a prototype Internet was in place and TCP/IP technology had been tested. At the beginning of 1983, ARPA expanded the Internet to include all the military sites that connected to the ARPANET. The date marked the transition for the Internet from an experiment to a useful network. During the decade 1983 to 1993 the Internet changed from a small experimental research project into the world's largest computer network. The number of computers connected to the Internet rose from a few hundred to over one million.

The early Internet was difficult to use only because of the lack of search engines.

Internet applications

The Internet has evolved a number of standard protocols. These include:

- FTP – file transfer protocol is the standard method of transferring files across the Internet.
- SMTP – simple mail transport protocol is an international standard for e-mail.
- HTTP – hypertext transfer protocol applies to a set of computers that provide information in a standardised form known as the World Wide Web.
- Webcast protocols – as well as providing text pages the World Wide Web now has webcast servers that provide continuously updating data including streaming audio and video.

The World Wide Web has a number of protocols that can be used on web pages. These include:

- HTML – hypertext mark-up language is the language behind most Web pages. It allows you to control how text and graphics are displayed. It also allows you to specify links to other pages.
- XML – extensible mark-up language is a development of HTML that provides additional facilities for use in e-commerce.
- Javascript – this is a cut-down version of the Java programming language that can be executed directly by web browsers.
- Java applets – these are small Java applications that can be executed via a web browser.

Java is a programming language that was developed by a company called SUN Microsystems.

Both Javascript programs and Java applets are very limited in what they can do.

Progress check

1 Protocols are used when networking computers. Explain what is meant by protocols and why they are necessary. [4]

2 Briefly describe **both** the application layer and the physical layer in the OSI seven-layer model. [2]

NEAB 1999, CP05

1 A protocol is a set of rules that are applied to computer networks. The rules will apply to both hardware and software and are used to control the transmission of data.

2 Application layer is the top layer of the OSI model. It provides network applications and is the level that determines when data are to be transmitted or received.

The physical layer determines the electrical connections and specifies how the signals will be organised.

Sample questions and model answers

1

(a) What is meant by *half-duplex* transmission? [2]

(a) Half-duplex means two way communication but only one way at any time.

(b) What is the function of a *modem*? [2]

(b) A modem converts the digital signals from the computer into analogue signals that are suitable to be transmitted over the ordinary telephone line. It also converts analogue signals from the telephone line into digital signals that can be understood by the computer.

(c) State **three** forms of communication, other than text, that can be transmitted through an Integrated Services Digital Network (ISDN). [3]

Any three of these will do.

(c) There are a number of forms of communication including:

audio
images
video
numerical data

(d) Why does using an ISDN telephone line to connect a computer into a wide area network eliminate the need for a modem? [1]

(d) A modem is not required as the line operates using digital signals.

AEB 1999, Paper 3

2

A wide area network (WAN) contains a gateway. Explain what is meant by the term *gateway* in this context. [2]

A gateway provides a link between two networks. It will provide access to another network, for example the Internet.

NEAB 1999, CP05

3

A computer programmer working from home wishes to set up a connection between her computer and her company's computer using a modem connected to an ordinary telephone line.

(a) Explain the term **modem**. [2]

(a) A modem converts the digital signals from the computer into analogue signals that are suitable to be transmitted over the ordinary telephone line. It also converts analogue signals from the telephone line into digital signals that can be understood by the computer.

(b) State **three** parameters that must be set in order to establish the communications link. [3]

Any three of the these would be sufficient

(b) The parameters that have to be set include:

Telephone number
Speed, which might be in the form of baud or bit rate
Size of data block
Type of parity
Number of stop bits
Protocol used
Port to be used.

Sample questions and model answers (continued)

(c) Factors such as line noise can lead to errors in data transmission. Describe **two** commonly used methods of error detection. [4]

There are a number of answers to this question. You only need to provide two of them.

(c) An echo check may be used. The data that is transmitted is returned to the sender. The sender can then check that it has not been altered.

An odd/even parity bit could be added to make the total number of 1s, including the parity bit, an odd/even number. This will allow detection of single bit errors.

A hamming code can be added to the data. This will allow any single-bit errors to be corrected.

A check sum can be added to the data. This will be calculated using a mathematical formula and can detect multi-bit errors.

A control total can be added. This will be the total of some numerical data that are being sent, for example the total number of items sent to a customer.

A hash total may be added. This is a meaningless total of some of the data sent, for example the total of some reference numbers.

A batch total can be added to a batch of data. This might be the total number of transactions.

(d) Her company operates a local area network consisting of 12 diskless workstations and a dedicated file server. One of the workstations also acts as a print server.

Explain **two** functions of each of the following:

(i) print server [2]

(d) (i) To enable workstations access to a shared printer.
To manage the printing.

(ii) file server. [2]

There are many answers to this question. Any of these would do.

(ii) To store applications.
To store user's files.
To allow shared access to files.
Remote booting.

These are the two main points. Other points that would get you marks are: the workstation must always be switched on: workstation could become unserviceable if the print server software fails

(e) State **two** possible disadvantages of using a workstation as a print server. [2]

(e) The workstation will be slowed down when it is busy printing.
The print server software will use up some of the memory leaving less for the workstation software.

(f) The company plans to install a multimedia server on this network.

(i) What is meant by multimedia? [2]

(f) (i) A combination of text, sound, images and video clips.

(ii) Give **three** reasons why the company's current hardware might not be suitable to run multimedia applications from this multimedia server. [3]

Again, there are a number of possible answers. Any three of these would do.

(ii) Bandwidth of the network cable might be insufficient.
Workstations might not have enough memory.
Workstations might not have sufficiently fast processors.
Workstations may have no sound capabilities.
Workstations may not have a suitable graphics card.
Workstations may have unsuitable monitors.

AEB 1998, Paper 3

Practice examination questions

1 (a) What is meant by a *wide area network*? [1]

(b) Explain the term *protocol* in the context of data transmission over a wide area network. [2]

(c) Why is a protocol needed for a wide area network? [1]

AEB 1999, Paper 3

2 Explain what is meant by:

(a) circuit switching [2]

(b) packet switching [2]

in communication networks.

NEAB 2000, CP05

3 (a) What is meant by a distributed system? [2]

(b) Describe **two** advantages to an organisation of using a distributed system. [4]

NEAB 1999, CP05

4 An organisation is considering installing either a bus or a ring network to link together the computers within its head office. The computers are all situated on a single floor of the building.

(a) Give **one** advantage of **each** method of linking the computers together. [2]

(b) To control the transmission of data, the bus network uses *collision detection* and the ring network uses *token passing*. Explain what is meant by the terms collision detection and token passing. [4]

NEAB 1998, CP05

5 When computers are communicating across a network, it is important to establish whether packet switching or circuit switching should be used. It is also used to establish a set of rules for the communication to be successful.

(a) (i) Describe packet switching and circuit switching. [4]

(ii) State **one** advantage of each type of switching. [2]

(b) Explain **one** reason why the set of rules to establish this communication is set up in a layered format. [2]

OCR 2000, Paper 1

continued overleaf

Practice examination questions (continued)

6 A secretarial agency is to implement a local area network of microcomputers within its main branch. The following two configurations have been suggested:

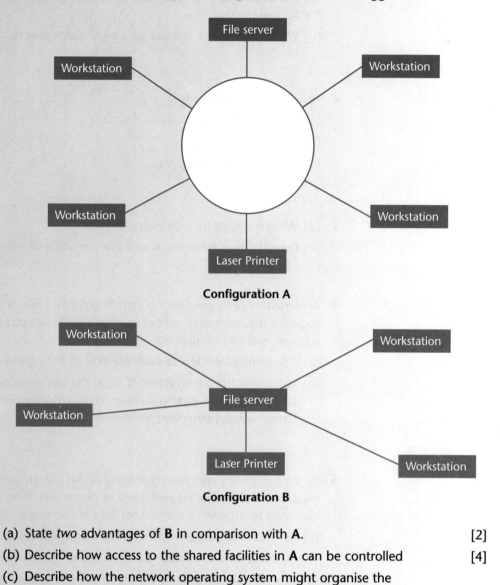

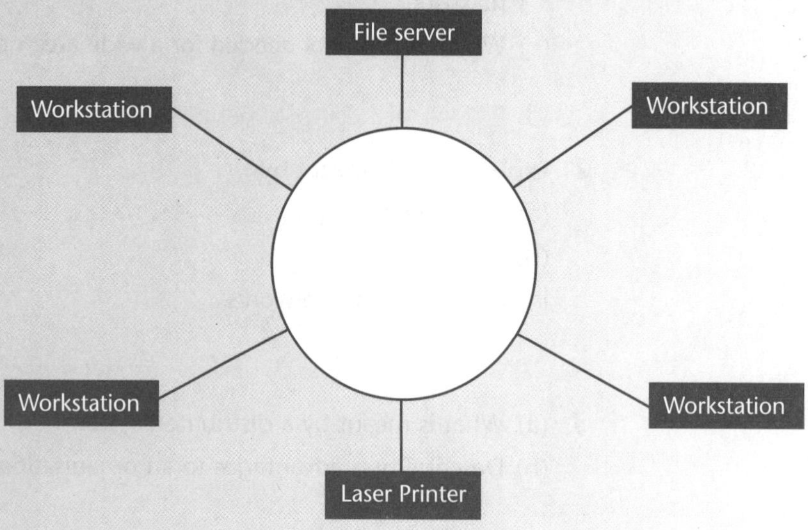

Configuration A

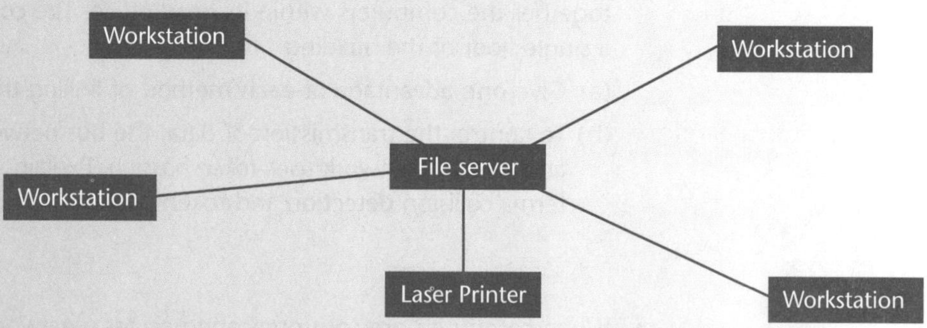

Configuration B

(a) State *two* advantages of **B** in comparison with **A**. [2]

(b) Describe how access to the shared facilities in **A** can be controlled [4]

(c) Describe how the network operating system might organise the communications between the file server and the workstations in **B**. [2]

EDEXCEL specimen

Chapter 10

Synoptic assessment

The Advanced Level criteria state that A Level specifications must include synoptic assessment representing at least 20% of the marks. Synoptic assessment is designed to test understanding of the connections between different elements of the subject. You may be asked to use your knowledge of various areas of the syllabus in order to solve a problem. This may be a situation where you are given a specification and you have to use your knowledge of hardware, software, networks, files and/or databases to produce a solution. Another area is where you are asked to discuss economic, social, legal and/or ethical issues and how they apply to computing. The project may be entirely synoptic and, in addition, there will be synoptic questions on the examination papers.

You need to be aware that questions are often synoptic and the examiner is looking for an answer that shows that you have taken account of the situation described in the question.

Sample questions and model answers

1

A local newspaper group produces local papers for five different areas. The five local offices feed material into the central head office. There are two editions per week, on Tuesday and on Friday. Each has some pages devoted to specifically local news, with the rest of the material being common to all.

In one of the local offices there are two terminals devoted to advertisements and five for reporters, all running the same specialised software package. A reporter can type in a story, using basic word-processing software, edit it and, when ready, send it down a *leased line* to the head office.

(a) (i) Why should a LAN be used within a local office? [1]

(a) (i) A LAN allows sharing of resources, e.g. a printer.

(ii) Why should a WAN be used between offices? [1]

(ii) The computers are spread over a wide area.

(iii) Draw a diagram to show a suitable network topology for the LAN. Your diagram should include a suitable position for the file server and the direction of data flow. [2]

(iii)

The diagram might be of a bus, ring or a star network.

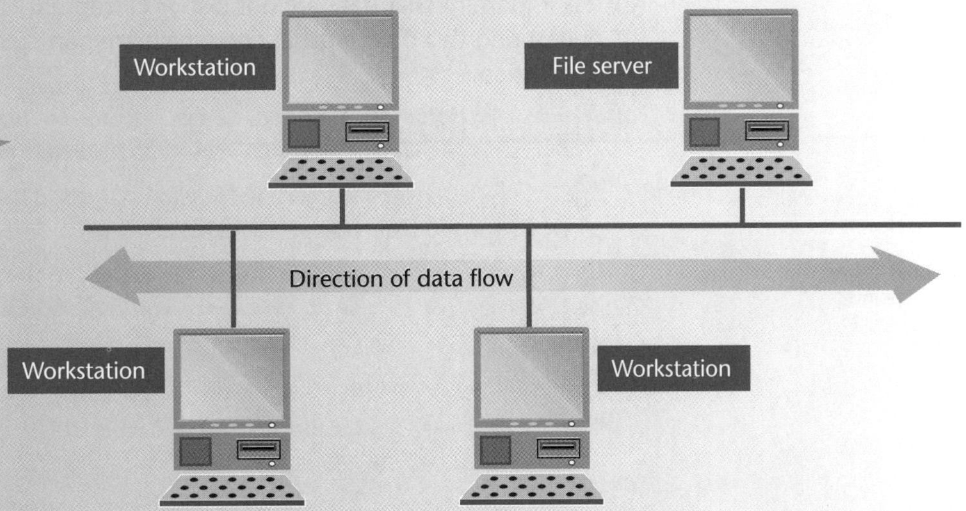

Sample questions and model answers (continued)

(iv) Give **one** advantage and **one** disadvantage of the topology you have described. [2]

(iv) The advantage of the bus is that it is simple and inexpensive to install as it uses the least cable.

The main disadvantage is that the performance degrades under heavy loads owing to collisions taking place.

Similar advantages and disadvantages apply to ring and star.

(v) Give **two** reasons for the use of a leased line. [2]

(v) Leased line always available.
More reliable transmission.
Allows a higher speed of transmission.
Can be more cost effective for large volumes of data.
It offers better security.

Any two of these will gain the marks.

(b) At the head office, the News Editor will use specialised desk top publishing software to combine the news stories from the local offices to build up a page, editing the stories as necessary. Pictures can be scanned in and placed appropriately. A laser printer is used to print the pages for proof reading.

(i) Describe and explain **one** type of editing that the News Editor would be likely to have to do to the stories, in addition to routine spelling and grammar checks. [2]

(b) (i) Parts could be deleted to make the story shorter to fit the space available.

Extra material could be added to make the story fit the space allocated.

The formatting could be altered, i.e. change the font and/or the size and shape of pictures to improve the presentation.

(ii) Describe carefully the process involved in scanning a picture and converting it into computer usable form. [4]

(ii) A light is shone on to the picture and the reflected light is measured. The picture is broken up into small pixels (or dots) and each dot is stored as a digital value in the memory of the computer.

(c) It is important that data are not lost or corrupted. Describe **two** distinct means of ensuring this does not happen which are particularly relevant to this application. [4]

(c) Frequent backups of the documents should be taken. These should be stored in a fireproof safe or removed to other premises in case of fire.

Anti-virus software should be applied to all data entering the system to prevent the system from being attacked by a virus.

Error correction technique should be used on the data transferred. The best method is to use a cyclic redundancy check.

Auto-save can be set on the editing software to prevent too much text being lost on computer failure.

The hard drives could be duplicated and the data written to both disks in case of hard-drive failure.

You could answer with any one of these points.

Sample questions and model answers (continued)

(d) Boxed advertisements are entered at two of the terminals in the local office. They are stored temporarily on the local file server, which is polled every thirty minutes by the central computer at head office when they are transmitted.

(i) They are then stored in a centralised database at head office having been given an advert_number as the key field. The next advert_number is automatically produced by the software and cannot be over-ridden. Explain carefully why the advert_number is produced in this way. [2]

(d) (i) It ensures a unique identifier when advertisements are being entered from many different offices.

(ii) When booking a boxed advertisement, the client has to specify not only the layout and wording required, but also practical details such as the size of the box, and whether the advert is to go in just once, or be repeated for a number of editions. The amount of detail specified will vary from one booking to the next. These advertisements could be stored in the database as fixed length or variable length records. Give one advantage for storing them as fixed length records and one advantage for storing them as variable length records. [2]

There are three points. Any one would do.

(ii) Fixed length records are simpler to process.
They can be updated in situ.
Accurate estimations of the disk space required can be calculated.

(e) Traditionally, all back copies of a newspaper are kept or archived. Suggest a suitable archiving medium for a local paper like the one described, and give two reasons why your suggestion would be the best medium to use for this purpose. [3]

Any one of these three will do.

(e) CD-R (or CD-RW) – this is inexpensive, compact, not easily corruptible.
Microfilm (or microfiche) – this is inexpensive, compact and not easily corruptible.
Magnetic tape (or cartridge tape or DAT) – this is inexpensive, has a large capacity and is robust.

(f) The Group is exploring the possibilities of using the Internet. Suggest two ways in which the Group could benefit from the Internet. [2]

Any two of these would do.

(f) The Internet could be used as follows:
To advertise.
The company could have its own website.
It could display the paper on the Internet.
It could use the Internet as a source of information.
It could receive advertisements over the Internet.

[Quality of language 3 marks]

AEB 1998, Paper 2

This question had 3 marks for quality of language. This is now common practice and the marks are likely to be: 1 mark for correct grammar, punctuation and spelling, 1 mark for clear and logically presented argument, 1 mark for using appropriate technical terms.

Sample questions and model answers *(continued)*

2

Passengers can telephone a railway company to obtain the times of trains between any two towns, and the price of tickets.

The calls are answered by operators. Each operator uses a terminal connected to the central computer.

(a) State **five** items of data which the operator will have to ask for. [2]

(a) Departure station
Arrival station
Date of travel
Time of arrival or departure
Rail cards held
Child/adult/senior citizen
Class of travel
Return/single.

> Any five of these will do, but do not include name, address, telephone number.

(b) Design an input screen format suitable for this application. [5]

(b)

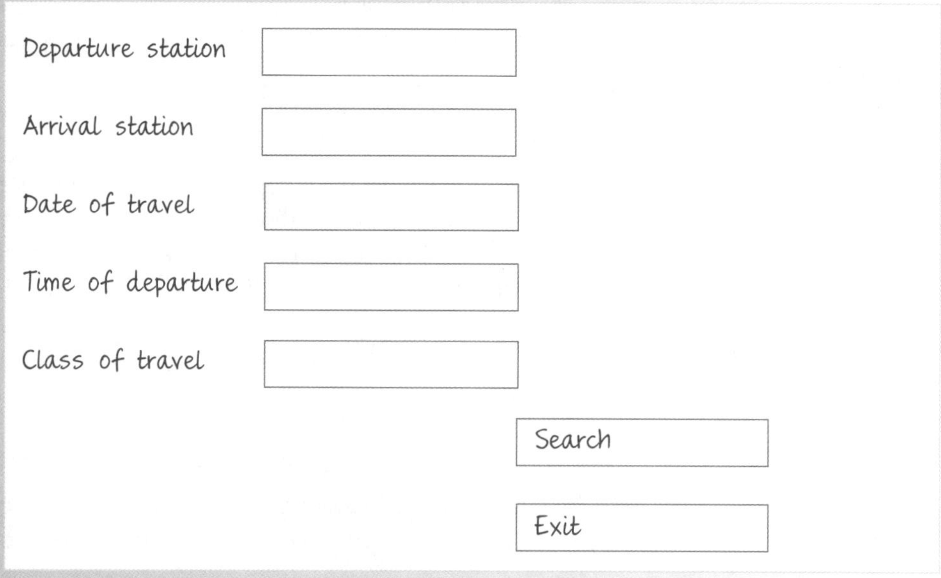

> Any suitably designed screen arranged logically will get you the marks. An example is illustrated.

(c) The operators work an eight-hour shift. Describe the requirements for a safe, healthy and efficient working environment for the operators. [4]

(c) Good lighting
Ergonomic furniture
Screened VDUs/low radiation monitor
Windows with blinds
Air conditioning/heating
Regular breaks etc.
Arm/wrist supports or ergonomic keyboards
Cables hidden.

> You will need to give four correct ideas. A selection is listed.

Sample questions and model answers (continued)

(d) The management of the railway company is considering making a similar system available on the Internet.

State **one** advantage and **one** disadvantage of such a system for:

(i) the passengers [2]

Be careful not to give the same point in both parts. For example, it is a disadvantage to both the passenger and the management that hardware must be obtained but you will get the mark for this point only once.

(d) (i) An advantage is that there is 24 hour access to queries. Another advantage is that the passenger can obtain a printout of the answer to the query.

A disadvantage is that it requires hardware/software to make the connection.

(ii) the management. [2]

(ii) An advantage is that it reduces the number of telephonists required.

A disadvantage is that it needs to be regularly updated. Another disadvantage is that the company will need to employ specialist staff.

EDEXCEL 1999, Paper 1

3

An example would do. You should supply a select statement of the type.

Your name Held 120 times in Government files

This headline in a newspaper is introducing an article on the large amount of data duplication in personal information held by official organisations.

(a) (i) Explain how a database could help to solve the problem of data duplication. [2]

(a) (i) Data can be stored only once in a database. Each person can be given an id and the data can be accessed through the id.

There are a number of reasons. Any two would be sufficient.

(ii) Give two reasons why people might be unhappy with this solution and explain in each case how their concerns might be eased. [4]

Any two from these will do

(ii) Lack of privacy – solution is to ensure adequate security.
Fear of 'police state' – solution is to have rules on who has access to the information.
People object to junk mail – solution is to prevent this use of the database.
Easy to connect different data sets – solution is additional security.

(b) Give an example of how a *query language* might be used in an application of this type, making it clear what the result of your query should be. [2]

(b) An example is from driving licence data. This picks out the drivers whose licence has almost expired.

SELECT driver_number WHERE (lic_number-current_date) LESS_THAN 30

(c) Explain briefly why primary key fields are so important in a database. [2]

(c) It is necessary to identify a record uniquely and this is the purpose of the primary key field.

WJEC CPS Specimen

Sample questions and model answers (continued)

4

A bank uses a batch processing system to print monthly statements for customers. Other computer applications may require different types of processing system to ensure that data are processed efficiently.

(a) Name **three** different processing systems and describe the main characteristics of each. [6]

(a) Transaction processing – processing each transaction as it occurs.
Real-time – processing of data so quickly that results are available to influence current activity.
Offline processing – not under the immediate control of the computer, e.g. data entry to disk.
Online processing – accessing data and creating transactions immediately.

Make sure that you read the question carefully. You will get no marks for batch processing.

(b) For each of the processing systems which you have named in your answer to part (a), briefly describe an application that is likely to use that processing system.

Justify the use of the particular processing system in each case. [6]

(b) Any transaction-based system, for example POS in a supermarket.
A real-time system such as air traffic control.
Offline could be collecting orders by a door-to-door salesperson.
Online processing might be a banking system using ATMs.

Automatic teller machines commonly known as cash dispensers.

(c) During the early stages of design, systems analysts have to make a decision about which processing system is the most appropriate for a particular application. Describe the effects that this decision is likely to have on:

(i) file design

(c) (i) Direct access will be required if the processing requires an immediate response.

(ii) hardware specification. [3]

(ii) A large fast hard-drive will be required for direct access with immediate response.

EDEXCEL 1999, Paper 1

Practice examination questions

1 The Museum of the Late Twentieth Century (MOLT) has built up a collection of objects intended to help to serve as reminders to future generations of important matters in the last two decades of the second millennium. It has many mechanical, electronic and image-based materials including interactive video as well as more conventional films and music.

MOLT is still expanding its collection, and is moving to new premises. It is planning what facilities and information services it should make available to users of the museum, both visiting and remote.

MOLT decides to produce an online 'Guide to Exhibits', to be used within the Museum on terminals specifically chosen and configured for the task.

(a) Describe and justify the hardware that would be required for this application. You should consider data storage, data communication and the user interface in your answer. [8]

(b) Describe **two** methods that can be used by visitors to the museum to find details about a particular subject, giving an advantage and a disadvantage of each. [8]

(c) Describe briefly the basic features of a data structure that would be suitable for storing the Guide. [8]

OCR 2511 Specimen

2 (a) The binary number 1000 0101 0011 can be interpreted in a number of different ways. State its value in denary if it represents:

(i) an unsigned binary integer [1]

(ii) a binary coded decimal integer [1]

(iii) a two's complement floating point number with an eight-bit mantissa followed by a four-bit exponent. [3]

(b) Express the denary number 31 in hexadecimal. [1]

(c) A recursively defined procedure B, which takes an integer as its single parameter, is defined below. The operators DIV and MOD perform integer arithmetic, x DIV y calculates how many times y fits exactly into x. x MOD y calculates the remainder that results. For example, 7 DIV 3 = 2 and 7 MOD 3=1.

```
PROCEDURE B (number)
   IF (number = 0) OR (number = 1)
      THEN PRINT number
      ELSE
         B(number DIV 2)
         PRINT number MOD 2
   ENDIF
END of B
```

(i) What is meant by recursively defined? [1]

(ii) Explain why a stack is necessary to execute procedure B recursively. [2]

(iii) Using a copy of the partially completed table shown below as an aid, dry-run the procedure call B(43) showing clearly the values of the parameter and the PRINTed output for the **six** calls of B.

Practice examination questions (continued)

Call number	Parameter
1	43
2	21
3	10
4	
5	
6	

[9]

(iv) What algorithm does procedure B describe? [2]

AEB 1998, Paper 3

Practice examination answers

Chapter 1 Applications

1 Pre-operation X-ray or ultrasound scans processed by computers.
Computer-controlled image processing passed from cameras inside the patient.
Robots can be used for precision operations.
Computer-controlled monitors for heart rate, blood pressure.
Training simulators to enhance the skill of surgeons.
[Any two of the above will do.]

2 Produce class lists at the beginning of the year for the form tutors.
Produce registers so that attendance can be recorded.
Create lists of examination entries to send to the examining boards.
Analyse attendance patterns using a spreadsheet.
Use the word-processor to produce information for parents.
Use a payroll program to calculate the pay of the staff of the school.
Use a word-processor to generate pupil reports.
Record student marks on a spreadsheet.
Use a timetable program to produce school timetables.
E-mail can be used to allow staff to communicate with each other.
Personal records of staff and students can be stored in a database.
A database or a spreadsheet can be used to record 'A' level choices.
[You would need to give a brief description of four of these to get the marks. Simply listing the item, e.g. 'registers', would not get you a mark.]

3 There are a large number of answers here. The important point is that you apply the use of simulation to an organisation. An example is a flight simulator. This is used to train pilots. The simulator will provide a mock-up of a real plane and will allow trainee pilots to learn how to operate the controls without leaving the ground. A good simulator will provide motion (by hydraulic rams on the simulator) and animated visual effects making the whole experience very realistic.

One advantage to the organisation is cost. It is much cheaper to operate a simulator than an aeroplane. It is also possible to generate a large number of dangerous situations on the simulator and this improves the quality of the training.

One advantage to society is that there are fewer planes flying around using up fuel and creating noise. It is also much safer for the public as pilots will fly only when they are properly trained.

4 The robotic vehicle could take still photographs or videos and it could take measurements of temperature, radiation, gravity, etc. It could collect geological samples and carry out analysis of them. The resulting data could be transmitted to earth for further analysis.

There are many advantages of using a robot vehicle. There would be no risk to human life. Also, the mission would be both cheaper and simpler. There is no requirement for life-support systems and there is no need to return to Earth.

There are some drawbacks. A robot is less flexible than a human. It would not be able to deal with unexpected problems and it may malfunction with little chance of repairing itself. It could easily get stuck (in a crater?) and be unable to free itself.

[7 marks are available for the content and 3 are awarded for the quality of the written communication.]

Chapter 2 Computer architecture

1 (a) (i) Increasing the width of the data bus allows more data to be transferred in one go. This will reduce the number of fetches required to obtain a complete instruction.
(ii) Increasing the clock rate reduces the time it takes to perform each operation so each fetch/execute cycle will be quicker.
(b) Pipelining allows the fetch to overlap the execute phase of the fetch/execute cycle.

2 (a)

		Input 1: 0	Input 1: 1
Input 2	0	0	1
	1	1	0

(b) (i)

X	10001011
K	<u>11100010</u>
Result	01101001

(ii) 10001011

3 (a) A signal from a device seeking the attention of the processor.
(b) A key is pressed on the keyboard
Disk has completed transfer
[or any other valid interrupt].

4 When base register addressing is used, all addresses in the program are regarded as offsets. An actual address is computed by adding an offset to the base register. In a multiprogramming environment, programs have to be located in different places in memory. When a program is loaded into memory the base register is loaded with the memory location of the start of the program. This allows a program to be located anywhere in the memory.

Chapter 3 Data representation

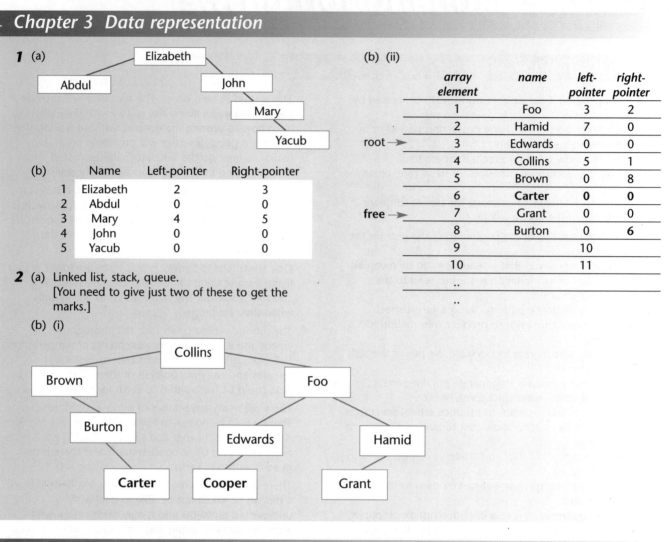

1 (a)

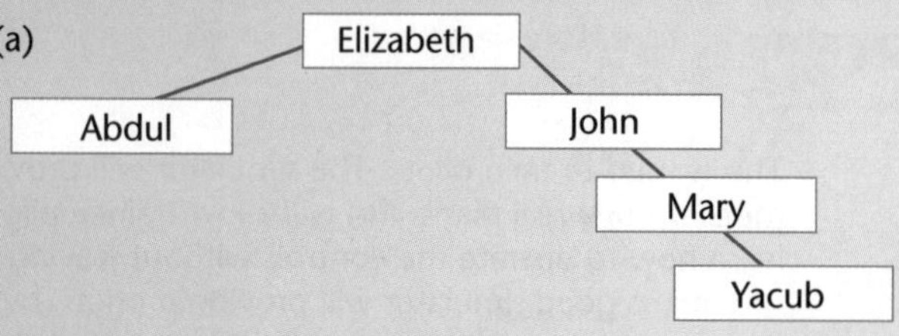

(b)

	Name	Left-pointer	Right-pointer
1	Elizabeth	2	3
2	Abdul	0	0
3	Mary	4	5
4	John	0	0
5	Yacub	0	0

2 (a) Linked list, stack, queue.
[You need to give just two of these to get the marks.]

(b) (i)

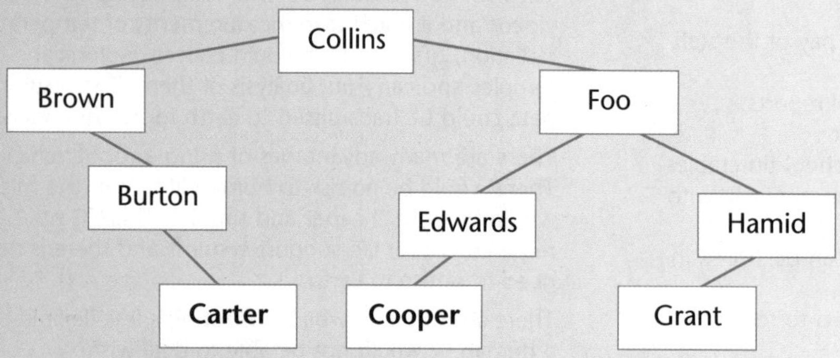

(b) (ii)

	array element	*name*	*left-pointer*	*right-pointer*
	1	Foo	3	2
	2	Hamid	7	0
root →	3	Edwards	0	0
	4	Collins	5	1
	5	Brown	0	8
	6	**Carter**	**0**	**0**
free →	7	Grant	0	0
	8	Burton	0	**6**
	9		10	
	10		11	
	..			
	..			

Chapter 4 Operating systems

1 File name
File type
File size
Creation date/time
File access status
(Read/Write/Hidden/System/Archive/etc.)
Address of first block
Date/time last altered
Date/time last accessed
Owner
Version/generation number
[You need to give just three from this list to get the marks.]

2 Virtual memory is a memory management technique. It specifies an amount of virtual memory that can be larger than the amount of physical memory. The hard disk is used to provide the virtual memory and blocks of program instructions (called pages) are loaded into physical memory as required. In this way, programs can be executed when they do not fit into physical memory.

3 Disk cache is memory that is allocated to the task of storing the last block of data read. When another read takes place it is likely that the data may be already in the cache. It takes less time to read from cache than from the disk so the process will be speeded up. It may also hold any indexes that are being used so that access to these will also be faster.

4 (a) When one program (say program A) wants a resource that another program (say program B) is using, it has to wait. If program B wants a resource that program A is already using, it will also have to wait. We now have a deadlock situation where neither program can proceed.

(b) (i) A will be loaded.
There are insufficient disk drives to load B.
C will be loaded.
There is insufficient memory to load D.
E will be loaded.

(ii) One of the currently running programs will have to finish.

(iii) If A finishes B will be loaded.
If C finishes D will be loaded.
If E finishes it is not possible to load any other program.

Chapter 4 Operating systems (continued)

5

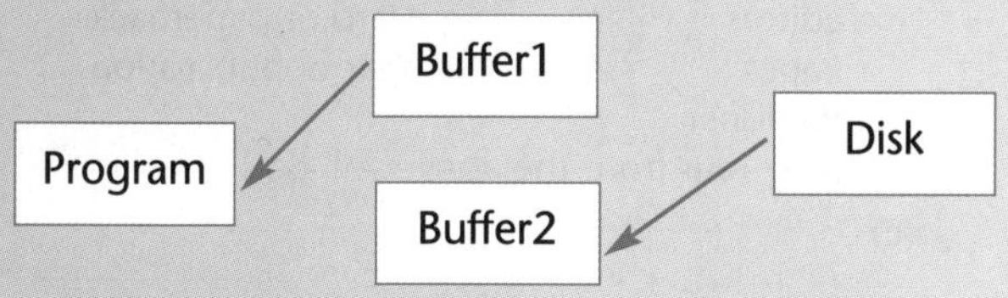

To transfer data from the disk to a program the following will take place:

- Data will be transferred from the disk to fill Buffer1.
- Data can now be transferred to the program from Buffer1. At the same time Buffer2 can be filled with data from the disk.
- The program can now remove data from Buffer2 while the disk refills Buffer1.

6 (a) The three states are:
Running
Waiting to run (Ready but blocked)
Suspended awaiting data transfer.

(b) (i) High priority is given to peripheral-bound programs. Low priority is given to processor-bound programs.

(ii) Peripherals are the slow part of the process. A peripheral-bound process will quickly release the processor and, while a slow data transfer takes place, a processor-bound process can use the processor.

Chapter 5 Files and databases

1 (a)

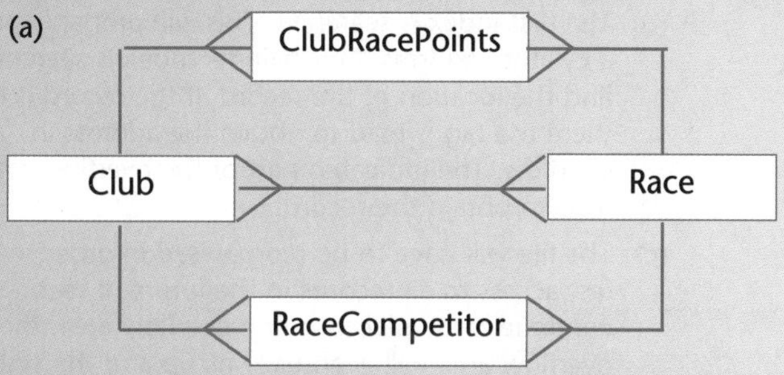

(b) (i) Race(<u>RaceIdNo</u>, Date, StartTime, DistanceCovered, Venue)

(ii) Club(<u>ClubName</u>, ResultsSecretaryName, Address, TelNo)

(iii) RaceCompetitor(<u>RaceIdNo, CompetitorNo</u>, CompetitorName, ClubName, RacePosition, RaceTime)

(iv) ClubRacePoints(<u>ClubName, RaceIdNo</u>, Points)

(c)
```
SELECT Position, CompetitorName, ClubName,
RaceTime
FROM RaceCompetitor
WHERE RaceIdNo = Given Race
ORDER BY Position
```

2 An indexed sequential file stores the data sequentially and has an associated index to allow direct access to the data. A multi-level index will have at least two levels of index. An example is a top-level cylinder index that holds details of which index holds a particular record. Each cylinder will contain a second-level index that will indicate the position of the records within the cylinder.

3 (a) (i) Address
Parental contact telephone number
Medical information
Date of birth
Subjects studied
[Any four relevant and distinct fields will do. The above are a few suggestions.]

(ii) Address
Home telephone number
Medical information
Qualifications
Subject taught
[Again, any four relevant and distinct fields will do. These are a few suggestions.]

(b) Students should not be able to change any data.

Students should not be able to read lecturers' personal details, e.g. telephone numbers.

A DBMS has built-in security features to control users' access to data.

(c) (i) Third normal form means that:

Data items are dependent on the key only.

Data items are dependent on the whole key.

(ii)

STUDENT Table

Student Number *	***Student Name***	***Tutor Number***
6137	Morton, Lynne	407
6153	Khan, Imran	410
6189	Evans, Elwyn	407
6192	Ho, Carol	408
6207	Vernon, Wayne	407
6208	Dodd, Debbie	414
6226	Evans, Elwyn	414
6228	Alton, Chris	407
6231	Mir, Razwana	425
...	...	...

Chapter 5 Files and databases (continued)

TUTOR Table

Tutor Number *	***Tutor Name***	***Tutor Room***
407	Harris, Dave	215
408	Jones, Christine	220
410	Adams, Jessica	214
414	Buckley, Ruth	215
425	Beaumont, Jim	214
…	…	…

* = key field

ROOM Table

Tutor Room *	***Tutor Telephone***
214	495
215	492
220	
…	…

4 (a) A database where the data are structured as a series of tables and the database management system provides tools for joining tables together and selecting items from within tables.

(b)

Barcode	Author
Location	Number of copies
Edition	Category
Size	Buying price
Weight	Selling price
Editors	Hard or paperback
Pages	Year of publication
Publisher	

[Any four from the above will do.]

(c)

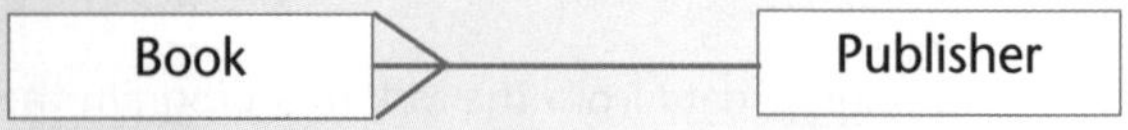

(d) Suggested answers are:

Entity	***Relationship***	***Key field***
Order	book identifier	order number
Customer	order identifier	customer id (or name+address)
Sales Person	sale identifier	staff number
Sale	order identifier	sale number

5 (a) There is a separate area for overflow records. When data are placed in overflow a tag is placed in the correct location for the record.

(b) The first index is searched. This will probably provide a cylinder address. The cylinder index is searched to find the location of the record. If the record is not there the tag is read to obtain the address in overflow. The indicated part of the overflow area is read to obtain the record.

(c) The file will have to be reorganised in order to allow fast access to all records in the future. If records continue to be placed in the overflow area, the overflow area will eventually fill up and the system will fail.

Chapter 6 Programming languages

1 (a) An interpreter translates one line then allows it to be run before translation of next line. A compiler translates the whole program as a unit and creates an executable program.

(b) (i) When program is to be run a number of times.
When the amount of memory used is not important.
When speed of execution of code is important.
[Any two of the above will do.]

(ii) When debugging a program.
When the size of the object code will cause problems of storage.
When a prototype is needed.
[Again, two of the above will get the marks.]

(c) Position from which procedure call is made is loaded on to stack with values of any parameters passed by reference. At the end of a call the return addresses and the parameters are removed from the top of the stack.

2 A translation error is a syntax error, for example a reserved word spelt incorrectly.
A linking error will be generated by a missing library program.
An execution error will be caused by an error such as divide by zero, infinite loop, file read error, etc.

3

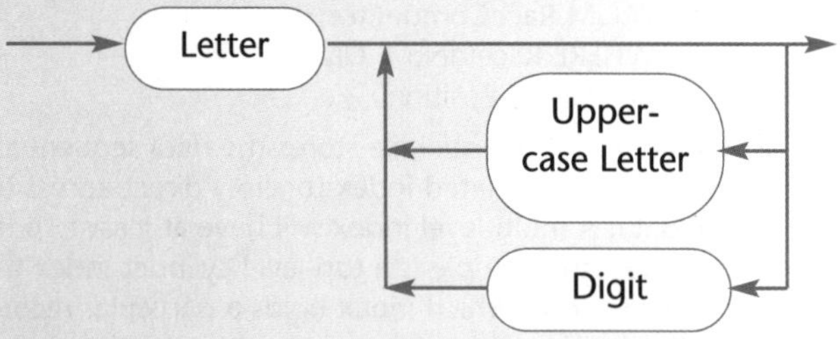

4 (a) answer = 35

(b) answer := i (e(y, 7), s(p(4,x),y), p(3,x))

5 (a) Syntax is the definition of valid sentences in a language.

(b) (i) All the clauses 1 to 9 are facts so any one of these will do.

(ii) All of the clauses 10 to 16 are rules so any one of these will do.

Chapter 6 Programming languages (continued)

(c) (i) The sentence is valid. The rules used are 16, 11, 13.

(ii) The sentence is valid. The rules used are 16, 11, 13.

(d) sentence(A,B,C,D,E,F,G) IF noun_phrase(A,B) AND verb_phrase(C) AND noun_phrase(D,E,F) AND adverb(G).

(e) (i) A programming language has a smaller vocabulary and fewer ways of constructing 'sentences'.

(ii) A lexical analyser includes the following functions:

groups character stream into syntactic units (i.e. key words)
creates tokens for further processing
creates the symbol table
removes white space (i.e. blanks, tabs, new lines, etc.)
removes comments
loads include files
keeps track of line numbers
produces an output listing.
[Any four of the above will get the marks.]

(iii) Even though the statement may be lexically and syntactically correct it may be semantically incorrect (i.e. it may not have a valid meaning). An example might be to assign a real value to an integer variable.

Chapter 7 Algorithms

1 (a)

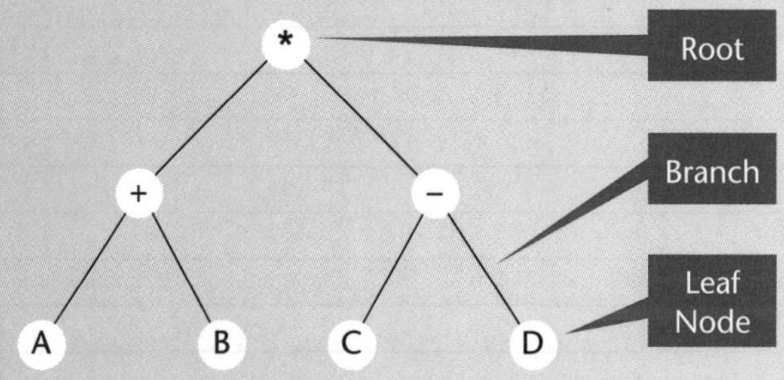

(b)

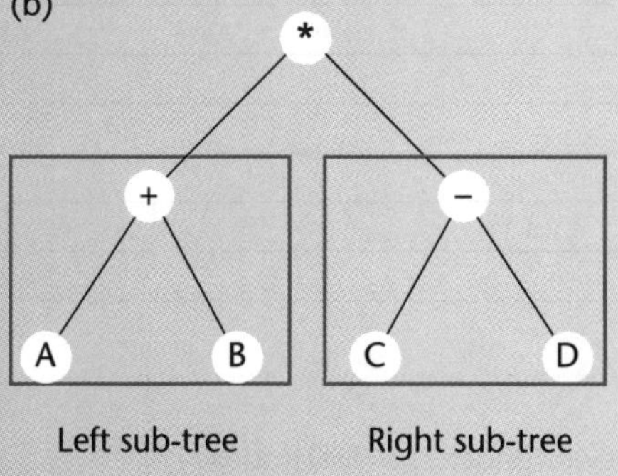

(c) A procedure that calls itself is said to be recursive.

(d) So that each call to T can pass a new value of the parameter.

(e)

Call number	*Parameter*
1	tree('*', tree('+', tree('A',empty,empty), tree('B',empty,empty)),tree('-', tree('C',empty,empty), tree('D',empty,empty)))
2	tree('+',tree('A',empty,empty), tree('B',empty,empty))
3	tree('A',empty,empty)
4	tree('B',empty,empty)
5	tree('-',tree('C',empty,empty),tree('D',empty,empty))
6	tree('C',empty,empty)
7	tree('D',empty,empty)

(A+B)*(C–D)

(f) In-order traversal.

Chapter 7 Algorithms (continued)

2 (a)

Comment	*Count*	*rp*	*max*	*cp*	*Temp*	*Numbers* 1	2	3
Global values on call			3			13	25	24
rp: = 1		1						
Repeat								
rp: = rp + 1		2						
cp: = 1				1				
while rp > cp do								
if numbers[rp] > numbers[cp] then								
temp:= numbers[rp]					25			
for count = rp to cp + 1 step –1	2							
numbers[count] := numbers[count –1]							13	
endfor	1							
numbers[cp] := temp						25		
endif								
cp := cp + 1				2				
endwhile								
until rp = max								
rp := rp + 1		3						
cp := 1				1				
while rp > cp do								
if numbers[rp] > numbers[cp] then								
endif								
cp := cp + 1				2				
endwhile								
if numbers[rp] > numbers[cp] then								
temp := numbers[rp]					24			
for count = rp to cp + 1 step –1	3							
numbers[count] := numbers[count–1]								13
endfor	2							
numbers[cp] := temp							24	
endif								
cp: = cp+1				3				
endwhile								
until rp = max								

(b) Insertion sort.

(c) To make space for an insertion would involve moving up to 500 items individually and this would take some time.

3 The algorithm can be simplified by adding terminators to the lists. A terminator will have a larger value than any existing item.

```
Add terminators to both lists
Index1 := 1    /* assuming that the list's first entry
is  in location 1 */
Index2 := 1
Index3 := 1
While list1[Index1] is not a terminator OR
list2[Index2] is not a terminator do
   IF list1[Index1] < list2[Index2] THEN
      newlist[Index3] := list1[Index1]
      increment Index1
   ELSE
      newlist[Index3] := list2[Index2]
      increment Index2
   ENDIF
   increment Index3
ENDWHILE
```

Chapter 8 Systems development

1 (a) MOLT would need to start with a model of the space and a crude initial design of the exhibits, use simulation to check out the feasibility of the design, use simulation results to suggest refinements and proceed to check the final design against actual experience when open to the public.

(b) MOLT could hire someone with expertise who would be under MOLT's control but slow.

MOLT could buy a package and learn how to use it. This is likely to be the cheapest but least likely to result in what they want.

MOLT could let a consultant do it. This is the most expensive, probably the least flexible but likely to produce the most professional result.

(c) The output must always include values of parameters, and be presented in a way that is appropriate for its content and for the audience.

The output will clearly show changes over time.

The details of layout using CAD graphics such as:

The speed of flow or traffic density using colour bars on a time line.

Bottlenecks or hazards using flashing video on screen.

(d) Testing when full of visitors.

Testing special-circumstance users such as disabled visitors.

Testing a normal day.

Testing emergency situations.

2 To confirm that appropriate techniques have been used.

To check correspondence between the design and the specification.

To confirm that the user interface is appropriate.

[Any two of the above will get the marks.]

3 (a) property – (propertyId, status, dateLastCleaned)

customer – (customerId, name, address, telNo, depositPaid, numberIn Party)

bookings – (bookingId, propertyId, customerId, date)

(b) The user interface will have icons for:

booking an apartment

entering customer details

shutting down the application

entering a date to check availability, etc.

(c) An example is the number of bookings in a particular month. To produce this report the start date and end date must be entered. Then, the software will check the status of each property for each week and count the total number of weeks booked.

[Any sensible report would do but you must describe how it is produced.]

Chapter 9 Networking

1 (a) A wide area network is a network connecting geographically remote sites using telephone lines or radio links.

(b) A protocol is a set of rules that are used when connecting different computers together in a wide area network.

(c) There must be a common standard or the different computers would not be able to communicate successfully.

2 A circuit is an established dedicated link between two devices. The data link remains as long as the circuit is connected.

A packet switching system transmits packets individually. Each packet can take its own route through the network.

3 (a) In a distributed system, computers are connected over some form of network. Distributed systems involve shared processing. It takes less time to do the work by sharing it out.

(b) The advantage of a distributed system is that remote access to data is provided and the data are available to workers' desktops.

Another advantage is that computing power is available to perform other tasks in each location.

[A third advantage is that it makes it possible to provide access to other networks, such as the Internet, to workers' desktops.]

4 (a) A bus system will use less cable.

The ring system will allow faster transmission.

(b) Collisions occur when two computers attached to a bus system attempt to transmit at the same time. The computers 'listen' to the bus while transmitting and if a collision occurs they stop transmitting and try again later when the bus is free.

A token is passed around a token ring system. When a computer wishes to transmit it has to wait for a free token. When a free token arrives it attaches the data to the token.

5 (a) (i) Packet switching splits message into standard-size chunks, called packets, that are placed on the network independently. The packets are routed individually through the network.

Circuit switching systems set up a circuit through the network and then the messages are transmitted along the circuit.

(ii) The advantage of packet switching is that there is no overhead in setting up a circuit.

The advantage of circuit switching is that

Chapter 9 Networking (continued)

messages do not have to be reassembled upon receipt.

(b) Layering allows the altering of the contents of one layer without altering the other layers.

6 (a) The advantages of B in comparison to A include:

The passing of messages from one workstation to another or from the file server to a workstation is more secure.
A fault in a link or a workstation does not affect the rest of the network.
The file server can prioritise and control the use of shared devices.
Variable transmission rates between the file server and each workstation are possible.
[Any two of the four would do.]

(b) Access to the shared facilities in A could be controlled in the following ways:

Packets of information are continually circulating in the closed loop.

When a message is to be sent from one device to a device which has facilities which are shared amongst the users, or vice versa, the device sending the message has to wait until a packet is received which is empty. The message may contain instructions to print a file, for example.

The message is incorporated into the packet and the full packet sent around the network. When the device that is to receive the message is ready, it accepts the packet of information.

(c) The network operating system might organise the communications between the file server and the workstations in B by means of polling, in which each workstation is repeatedly interrogated in turn to establish whether it is holding data for transmission. In this situation, polling includes the process of collecting the data.

Chapter 10 Synoptic assessment

1 (a) MOLT will need a server with a file store and some extension of simple file handling (e.g. direct access of CD ROM and hard drive). PCs or terminals with network cards will be required to connect to the network. Sound cards will be required in order to produce audio output. The network will require cable to transmit the signals. This is likely to be twisted pair. An input device will be required that can be used by the customers. A good method would be a touch-screen as this can display the instructions and does not need skill to use. It has no moving parts and so is likely to be able to take some abuse. For output there will need to be screens to display data, speakers to produce sound, and printers to produce hard copy.

(b) A menu system in the form of a tree could be provided. The top-level choices lead to progressively more specialised lower levels. This is easily applied to a touch-screen but the user needs to know something about the thing being searched for.

The user could enter a keyword. This could be typed in or selected from list. This leads directly to the information but it can be difficult to find relevant keyword.

The user could find the information through a related topic. They could then use hot keys or hypertext to find the information. There is the advantage that this may lead to other information en route but it is somewhat down to luck that appropriate links exist.

There could be a free-text search. This searches for references throughout text rather than in an index. This captures all the references but it can be very time consuming and may give many spurious references.

[Any two of the above will get full marks.]

(c) A multi-keyed database could be arranged as indexed sequential files. Use could be made of secondary keys, keys arranged in multiple tables and/or pointers within data areas providing hypertext links.

2 (a) (i) 2131

(ii) 853

(iii) $-7\ ^{11}/_{16}$ or -7.6875

(b) 1F

(c) (i) A procedure that calls itself is defined as recursive.

(ii) It is necessary to store the values of the parameters and the return address each time the procedure is called.

(iii)

Call number	*Parameter*
1	43
2	21
3	10
4	5
5	2
6	1

Printed output is 101011

(iv) Converts denary to binary.

Index